THE MEDIEVAL ESTABLISHMENT

Designed as an introductory volume to medieval subjects in the PICTORIAL SOURCES SERIES, this title examines one of the keys to understanding the period 1200–1500, "authority." It studies the way in which many of the old forms of authority in church and state were placed under heavy strain, and looks at some of the new forms of authority which developed by their side in the wake of the twelfth-century Renaissance.

Using an extensive range of illustrative source material, from illuminated manuscripts, woodcuts, tapestries, coinage, woodcarvings, stained glass windows, banners, and other material, the author portrays these many changes in Chapters on: the medieval church and its religious, legal, and educational authority; lords and kings and the authority exercised through feudal landholding and the manorial courts; kingship and its specifically military and judicial authority; and the new merchant classes—a new and special feature of the period—through a study of the authoritarian guild system, and the "masterpiece" tests by which apprentices and journeymen hoped to join the mercantile establishment.

Geoffrey Hindley shows how these various forms of authority interacted upon each other—for example the effect of kingship and of the church upon mercantile usages, and shows the effect of each upon every class of society, nobility, priests, merchants, artisans, smallholders, burgesses, society's down-and-out, and those in England and elsewhere who rose in revolt.

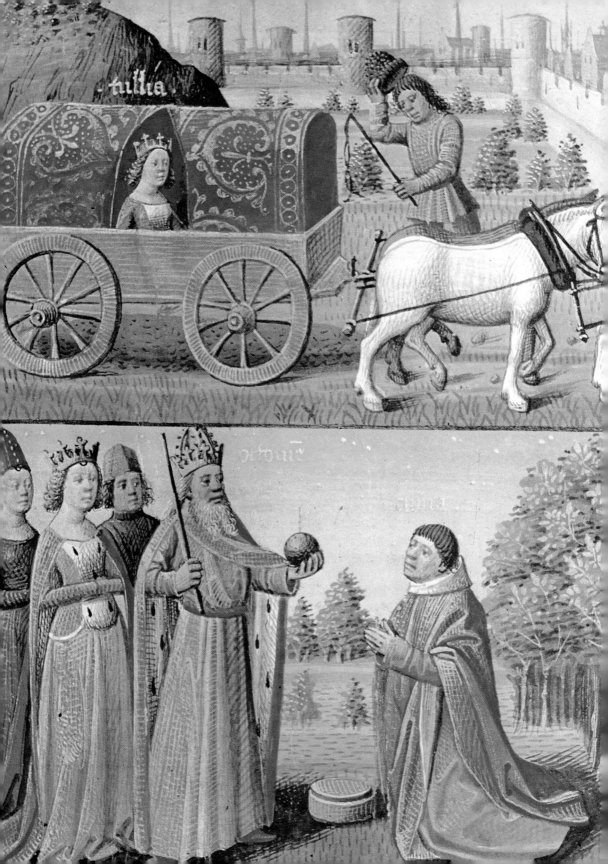

THE PUTNAM PICTORIAL SOURCES SERIES

THE MEDIEVAL ESTABLISHMENT

1200–1500

GEOFFREY HINDLEY

G. P. PUTNAM'S SONS · NEW YORK

The Putnam Pictorial Sources Series

Voyages of Discovery   G. R. CRONE AND A. KENDALL
The French Revolution   DOUGLAS JOHNSON
Shakespeare's England   LEVI FOX
The American Revolution   ROGER PARKINSON
The Dawn of Man   VINCENT MEGAW & RHYS JONES
Twentieth Century China   JOHN ROBOTTOM
Medieval Warfare   GEOFFREY HINDLEY
The Russian Revolution   LIONEL KOCHAN
The American Civil War   KEITH ELLIS

CONTENTS

CHAPTER ONE

AGE OF FAITH

IT IS PERHAPS because church authority loomed so large in everyone's lives that the period 1200–1500 is sometimes called the Age of Faith. The Christian ethic held a far stronger place in public life than it does in modern society. Yet when one seeks to find out exactly when religion held most sway, the answer retreats like a will-o'-the-wisp. For then as now, daily affairs were filled with political expediency, religious intolerance, and dissent and corruption in high places.

Yet the landmarks in those days were different. Among the bastions of authority, the great cathedral or monastery was just as important as the towering castle. Alongside the royal and secular courts ran a system of church or canon law, which sometimes fell into conflict with it. A tenant's landlord was as likely to be a monastic house or bishop as a lay nobleman. So great was the power of the church that even kings feared to be expelled from the fold, by excommunication. In an age, too, when marriage between powerful ruling houses played a major part in politics, the church stood above all. The pope's willingness to permit marriages between remote blood relatives became a matter of intense political concern.

Human nature itself may change little from one generation to another. Yet we can see that the actual organs of authority that governed medieval life and the principles behind them were very different from those of today. In recent years, the collective term "establishment" has been coined. The term describes those people and organizations—press, aristocracy, churchmen, politicians, bankers, leaders of industry—who are felt to hold the reins of power, who control the sources of news and shape public attitudes. This book, then, is about the medieval establishment as it existed between the years 1200 and 1500.

These were centuries of profound change. At the start of our period, high European politics were conducted in the shadow of two great concepts of an earlier age: the empire and the papacy. The Holy Roman Empire made claims to universal dominion. Its theorists traced its authority right back to the Roman emperors of the West. This secular claim was combined with a religious one, too. The empire, it was said, represented the authority of God in the secular world, just as the pope is seen as His vicar (deputy) in spiritual affairs. Grand though these claims were, they had to be made good in everyday politics.

The power of the medieval empire was founded upon the lands of the German kings who, during the eleventh and twelfth centuries, had been the most powerful rulers in Europe. They claimed to be the heirs of ancient Rome and aimed at incorporating northern Italy in their dominions and by being triumphantly crowned in the city of Rome itself. But the fact that their coronations were conducted by the pope, with brilliant ceremonial, was a sign that the papacy endangered their universal claims.

The conflict between empire and papacy, a classic theme of medieval history, reached its climax in the first fifty years of the thirteenth century. The final triumph of the pope was now made certain, for the death of the Emperor Frederick II in 1250 was followed by nearly thirty turbulent years, known as the Great Interregnum. During this time, the imperial throne was rocked by the fierce rivalry between several claimants, among them the Englishman Duke Richard of Cornwall. In competing for the support of the German princes, these rivals destroyed the authority of the very office that they fought for. The German lands finally disintegrated into a number of small, virtually independent states.

The church had defeated its great rivals, yet it had suffered serious losses of prestige. It had, after all, been a political battle. The great spiritual power of the church was debased by the use to which it had been put. The terror of excommunication, intended to keep men to the faith, was launched against Christian princes who came into political conflict with the church. At one time the pope even sponsored a military crusade against the emperor.

Even in the Middle Ages, some men were claiming that the seeds of church corruption had been sown long ago, when the Roman emperors had adopted Christianity in the fourth century. Such opinions did not, of course go unpunished. But the church's growing involvement in politics helped cause a decline in its authority, long before the Reformation of the sixteenth century. This decline was hastened by the Great Schism, when the church was torn between the rival claims of two—even three—popes. The schism, which lasted for some thirty years, was finally healed at the Council of Constance in 1415. These years had witnessed a heavy attack on the ideas of the papacy as a kind of spiritual monarchy. It seemed that the whole church establishment might be revolutionized and the pope made subject to a regular council of the church. The papal party was able to avert this threat to its position, but the fifteenth century saw the creation of the first national church in Europe to exclude papal power. This was the short-lived Hussite Church in Bohemia, which may be regarded as the forerunner of the Reformed Protestant national churches of the next century.

By the year 1500, therefore the two main pillars of the earlier medieval establishment had become gravely weakened. Let us look now at the bottom of the social scale. Whatever the fate of pope or emperor, the ordinary man still had to reckon with the power of bishop, king, or prince in his daily life. The influence of these figures was weakened less by events in faraway Rome than by local or national politics. They were threatened, too, by a force new to Europe —the self-governing town. In Chapter Three we shall look in closer detail at the rise of the merchant classes. We shall see how they won a new position of authority in European life, in one of the most radical changes in the establishment of the time.

Within our period, kings and princes had moved far toward consolidating their power. The idea of the sovereign nation state is a basic part of our political system today. It is perhaps difficult to think our way back into a world where kings sometimes fought with words and weapons to maintain their sovereignty against universalist claims of pope or emperor. Beneath the king all his subjects, high and low, stood in a clear social order. Bound by military and economic duties which arose from land tenure, their obedience was enforced by a variety of courts held by noblemen. The most coveted position in this order was that of a tenant in chief. Such a man held his land as a direct tenant of the king and owed obligations to no one else. Generally, tenants in chief were wealthy and powerful nobles. Most Europeans at the beginning of the thirteenth century owed their obligations to a local magnate and only indirectly through him to the king. In this situation, constant struggle took place between monarchs and their magnates; the king

sought to guarantee a supreme royal justice available to all subjects, regardless of intermediate feudal obligations. The lords resisted these encroachments on their power over their tenants. Eventually, the battle was won by the kings. The kings, however, were also having to fight against the claims of papacy and empire to rule in affairs secular and spiritual.

Papal claims were only finally overthrown at the Reformation, and even the idea of the empire died hard. Richard I of England, for example, had accepted the overlordship of the German emperor as the price of being set free from an imperial prison. Such was the length of legal memory that when the Emperor Sigismund visited England during the reign of Henry V, Duke Humphrey of Gloucester rode into the sea with drawn sword to demand that Sigismund should renounce the claims of his ancestors over the realm of England, before leaving the ship. In France, too, the monarch was determined to reject all superior claims. In the early fourteenth century, supporters of the French king made elaborate legal arguments to support his claim to be "emperor" within his own dominions. Even kings, then, heads of the feudal hierarchy, might feel themselves subject to higher authorities or claims. They fought or ignored these as the occasion might demand.

Below the kings, their own vassals continually tried to evade the obligations laid on them by feudal duty. Perhaps the nearest thing modern society has to feudal obligations is tax liability. Few people deny their duty to pay taxes, but endless ingenuity is used to reduce the amount due. In the same way, no vassal doubted that feudal obligation existed and bound him; however, many disputes and sometimes rebellions arose on the exact extent of that obligation. In the last resort, a great lord might not be too defiant towards royal authority. After all, his own position rested on the willingness of his vassals to acknowledge their feudal dues to him.

One might say that enlightened self-interest often bound the medieval establishment together, despite severe conflicts of interest within it. But for the ordinary man at the bottom of the social heap, such conflicts, even when they exploded into civil war, had little effect on his obligations. He still had to work on his lord's land, to pay for the privilege of having his wheat ground in the lord's mill, to attend at the lord's court or, for his bad conduct, at the church court. The medieval establishment drew its wealth and power from its humblest subjects, and hence the last Chapter of this book is devoted to the "common people". But first we turn to the power of the church, the pillar of this age of faith.

For the men of the time, the Church and its agents were all around. Even today the physical presence of the medieval church remains. The great churches and cathedrals of the Romanesque and Gothic Ages are landmarks of modern Europe.

The revival of medieval Christianity was marked by the founding of the Abbey of Cluny in the French province of Burgundy in the early tenth century. The gathering impetus of revival, 150 years later, revivified the papacy, and through it the clergy in general.

From the mid-eleventh century, every great European town was at one time or another in the throes of major building operations. These engrossed the energies of the whole community and were directed to raising the magnificent cathedrals that were the seats of power

1

2

3

4

for the bishops who represented the full panoply of the church's power in the world (1, 2, 3). A major event was the building of Chartres Cathedral. This so fired the imagination of people of all classes that noblemen and their ladies came to the site and helped the day workers in the hauling of stones and other materials used by the masons in this great monument to the glory of god (4, 5). Yet such a spirit of dedication, if not unique, was rare even in the Middle Ages, and some ambitious projects remained unfinished through lack of funds. But many were completed, and others were rebuilt more than once to satisfy the tastes of a new ecclesiastical patron. If economic investment is a measure of social values, how great was the medieval church that could mobilize such resources?

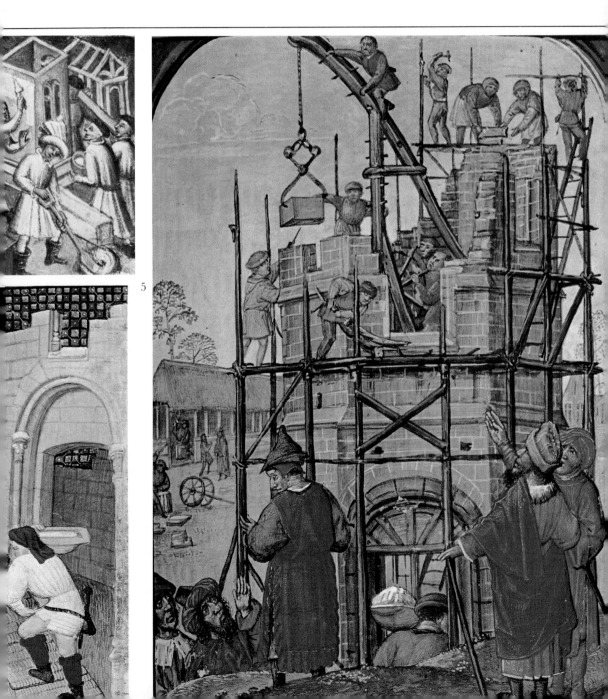

5

12 Western monasticism has in the early centuries respected the ideal of the hermits but the rule of St. Benedict, written in the sixth century, had shown the way to the union of the active and contemplative life. Depicted below are the foundation of an English abbey and the blessing of its charter (6) and a new monk receiving the tonsure (7). Later the monastic principle of obedience, poverty, and chastity in the service of God had been corrupted. Not only had many abbeys been founded by rich aristocrats, but noblemen themselves had become abbots and, in the process, helped to secularize the monastic ideal. Even Cluny in its turn became lax, acquiring wealth and losing its austere simplicity.

The next great reform of monasticism began at the Cluniac abbey of Cîteaux which under its abbot, St. Stephen Harding, in the early

6

7

8

twelfth century became the head of one of the greatest religious movements in European history. The Cistercians chose remote and inhospitable districts for their foundations and made the tilling of the land a central part of their daily rule. They came to engage lay brothers, subject to a less strict rule, to help them on their huge farms.

On the frontiers of Germany and in the remote parts of France they brought thousands of acres into cultivation, while in England such famous houses as Fountains Abbey became major wool producers. The Cistercians' devotion to honest toil sprang from their desire to shun the idle luxury into which the Cluniacs had fallen. But in time they, too, became wealthy and worldly landowners. A monk is shown instructing his brothers (8) and an abbot writing a manuscript in different inks (9), which was usually the task of a monk.

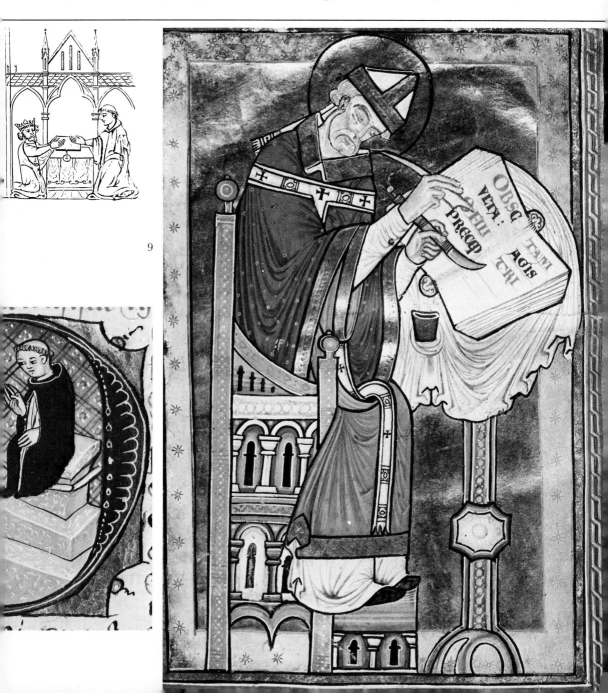

9

14 The busy and self-enriching industry of the monasteries enabled their well-protected monks to enjoy the delights of good hunting and the best of food and drink (12). This picture of a rich monk with his horse and hounds comes from an early manuscript of Chaucer's *Canterbury Tales* (10). Their wealth may have brought them into the charmed circle of the powerful, but it was at the price of mounting criticism. Here was a be-trayal of the example set generations before by holy men and hermits like St. Jerome (14). In the thirteenth century two new orders were founded, the Franciscans and the Dominicans. These came to be known as the mendicants because their founders forbade the ownership of property; their members were called friars like the character in the *Canterbury Tales* (11). The Franciscan order was founded by the saintly and humble St. Francis, the Dominican

10

11

13   12

by the more dynamic and scholarly St. Dominic. Whereas the monks had lived in great houses remote from the community they served and came to dominate, the friars entered the outside world. They were Europe's own missionaries. The Dominicans, indeed, became officially known as the Order of Preachers, and throughout the later Middle Ages the preaching of wandering friars (13, 15) was one of the most influential means of spreading the Christian message. Below (16), a French friar preaches to townspeople in the fifteenth century. The friars, who often preached without the permission of the bishop of the diocese, were despised for their poverty and disliked for their independence by the ecclesiastical establishment. But in at least one case, that of the Dominicans, the friars became very much part of the system being first appointed to begin the Inquisition.

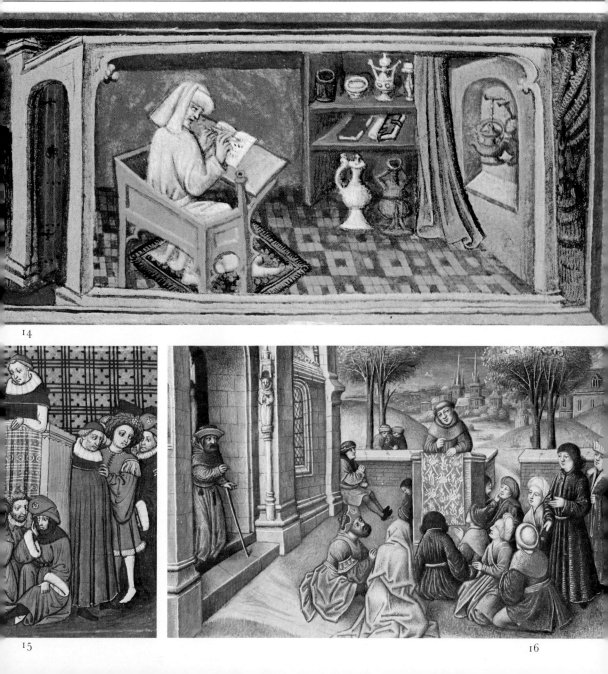

14

15

16

Few aspects of medieval religion are stranger to the modern mind than the cult of saintly relics. The veneration for relics encouraged by the great religious foundations certainly added to church prestige and tightened its hold on men's minds. Figure (17) shows a thirteenth-century English shrine being carried in procession before a king while crippled beggars prostrate themselves before it hoping for a cure. This drawing perfectly illustrates the point. Of course, the simpleminded were impressed, but in truth every class of society participated in the veneration of relics (18). One recalls the Canterbury pilgrims pictured here dining at an inn (22). Chaucer's Cook (19), Miller (20), and Friar (21) were all

17

19

20

18

drawn from real life. The obsession of King Louis XI of France with his vast collection of relics embarrassed even his courtiers. The church establishment was not always at ease about this cult, which seemed to imply that bones and fragments of dubious authenticity had more virtue than the rites of the church.

A vast flood of relics was released onto the European market after the sack of Constantinople by the Fourth Crusade of 1204. This thriving trade produced a comfortable income for a host of palmers and pardoners. (Palmers were pilgrims or monks who brought back palm branches or leaves from the Holy Land; pardoners were those who claimed to hold a papal licence to sell pardons or indulgences.)

21

22

The great churches of Europe, such as Santiago de Compostela, which claimed to have the body of St. James, one of the Disciples, and Canterbury Cathedral, which actually did have the body of St. Thomas à Becket, grew very rich from the offerings of pilgrims who came often immense distances to pay their homage to the saints. (See the illustrations of the Canterbury pilgrims on pages 16, 17.) Each of the churches in France that lay on the route to Santiago had its own relics so that the pilgrims could follow a special circuit. The whole institution of the medieval pilgrimage produced a large and continuous movement along the roads of Europe of all classes of society; undoubtedly the spiritual benefits expected from such journeys were important as incentives, but equally well the travel to strange lands itself was a powerful lure. Chaucer's Canterbury pilgrims like the Wife

25

26

23

24

of Bath (23), the Clerk (24), and the Squire (25) were certainly on the road as much to enjoy the delights of spring as to "seek the holy blissful martyr." Figure (29) is a satirical picture of a pious pilgrim seeing a flattering reflection of himself in a mirror.

On pilgrimage the great might mingle with the lower orders, as did Chaucer's worthy Knight (26), but generally, even in the affairs of religion, great men expected to be served by the high members of the church. When Louis, heir to Philip II of France, was taken to be healed by the relics of St. Denis, two robed bishops bore the precious remains of the saint before him (28). When King John of Portugal married John of Gaunt's daughter, the service was of course conducted by a bishop who also attended the festivities (27). In these ways, the great spiritual lords, lay lords and kings were closely linked together.

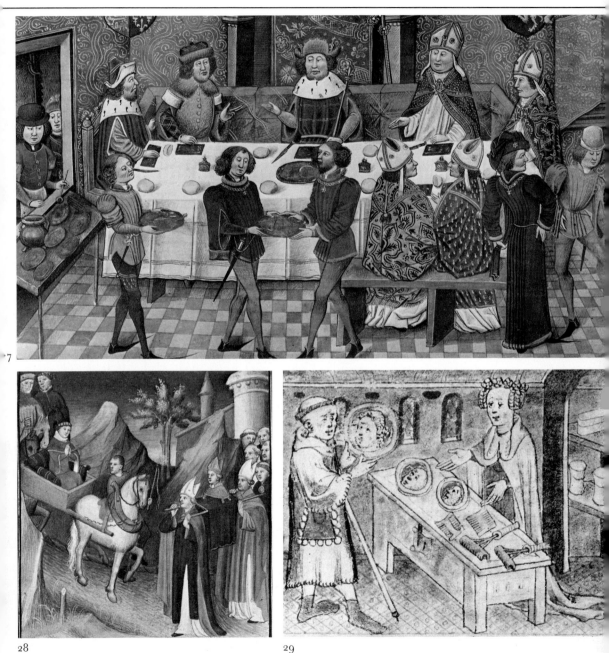

27

28

29

20 The power of the church in the lives of men was great and was often resented. In times of social unrest great abbeys, such as that at St. Albans, were liable to be attacked by angry mobs seeking to destroy the manorial records that held the details of their duties as tenants. But at all times the influence of religion was deep and real. Within days of birth the child was inducted as a member of Christ's body by baptism (30, 31) and washed clean of the stain of original sin with which it had entered the world. The rite was not an empty one; a child who died unbaptized, it was believed, was condemned to the pains of purgatory. At death men and women received the last rites of the church (32, 33) if they wished to be assured of avoiding the terrors of hell, and they were laid to rest in the consecrated ground of the churchyard, as in this Flemish woodcut of 1498 (34). For the great this last journey

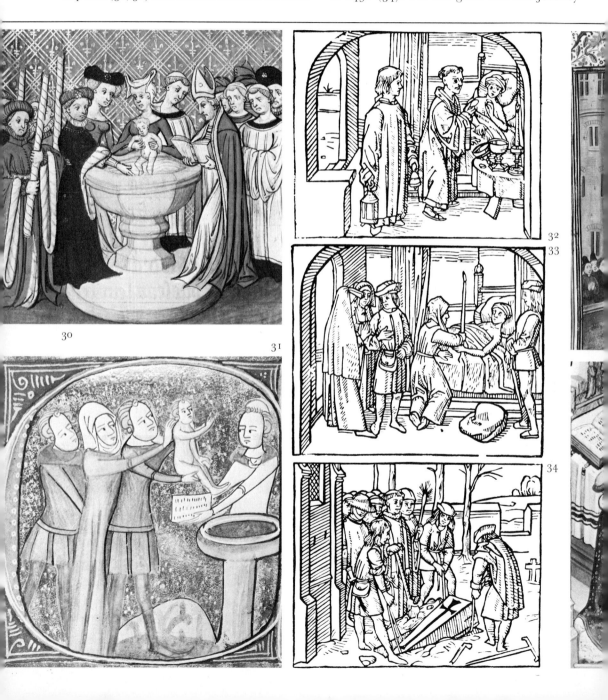

30

31

32
33

34

was surrounded with all the trappings of their grandeur in life (35), but even the glory of kings was subordinate to the blessing of the church.

By the twelfth century the church had made good its claims that, without its blessing, even marriage (37, 38), for long held to be a civil ceremony which required only the plighting of the troth of the contracting parties, was invalid. At all the turning points of life stood the church; this gave the ecclesiastical authorities considerable power. But at the heart of this power lay a mysterious, almost magical, function of the priestly office—the celebration of mass (36), and the miracle of the transubstantiation of bread and wine into the body of Christ Himself, the guardian of eternal life. Rich vestments, incense, and music (39) were all used to heighten the mystery and power of the service.

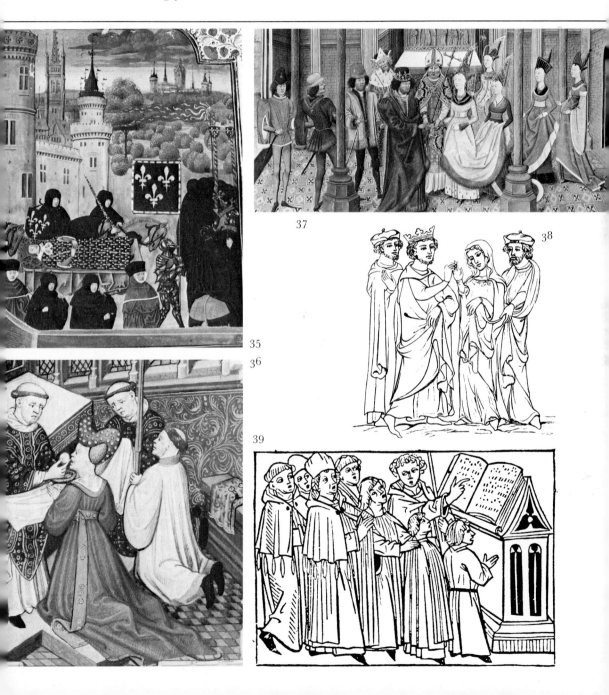

37

38

35

36

39

The design of medieval churches emphasized the mystery of the priestly office. The chancel, where the service was conducted by priests and choir, was screened from the public (40). The doctrine of transubstantiation conferred almost godlike powers on every priest, no matter how humble; it was crucial to the power of the church. The celebration of mass (42) was its sustaining act, and the fear of eternal hell the church's sanction (45).

Nuns (42), the female equivalents of monks, were, like all women of the time kept in their places, and though individuals may have had influence in the church, they were never allowed much authority.

The church courts held sway in all matters of moral delinquency from the arch "thought" crime of heresy to the more common peccadilloes like adultery (44). The activities of the medieval Inquisition, founded in 1233, are

40

41

42

43

often confused with the horrors of the state-run Spanish Inquisition founded at the end of the fifteenth century; those of the medieval Inquisition were not so horrendous, but they could be horrible enough. When all the evidence of informers had been taken and all the arts of persuasion and torture had failed, the offender was handed over to the civil authorities for burning alive (43). Human death was followed by the mercy of God. The system at its worst matched any modern police state. It was a healthy reminder of the power of the church. Nor was the secular establishment averse to using it for its own ends. The worst example was the destruction of the order of the Knights Templar by Philip the Fair of France, who coveted their immense wealth. The royal agents procured their executions on the pretexts of heresy and immorality.

44

Philip of France had to force the pope to acquiesce in his violence against the Templars, but as often as not, state and church worked in harmony. When they did come into conflict, the churchmen could usually hold their own. A more serious threat to the religious establishment was that posed by heresy and indeed by free thought in almost any form.

Ironically the church had kept alive the intellectual activity of Europe during the disordered centuries that followed the collapse of the Roman order. In the comparatively stable world of the twelfth century, when Europe witnessed a great intellectual awakening, scholars began to pose questions that went to the heart of the dogmas of religion. A great contribution to European culture was made by the countless monks who, often unable themselves to understand the great pagan classics, nevertheless hand copied them and

48

49

46

47

so passed down much classical literature to later generations (46, 47). But for a long time the only literate men in European society were churchmen. This monopoly of books and learning (48) greatly helped the church's attempts to control thinking. The first great schools were those attached to the cathedrals, such as that at Chartres, but from the late twelfth century on, "student power" began to take a hand. Inspired by brilliant and unorthodox masters like Peter Abelard, the newly formed universities began to acquire a life and tradition of their own that often conflicted with the church nominally at their head. Pictures (49, 50, 51) show scholars and pupils working from manuscripts and (52) German students working from printed texts in the year 1490. The principal subjects of study included theology, grammar, logic, and rhetoric.

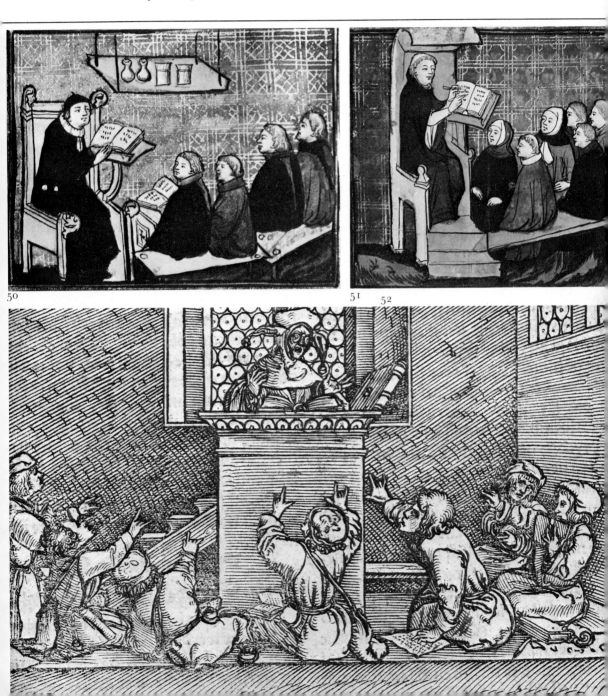

50

51   52

The University of Paris, the intellectual capital of Europe, was the most distinguished. It also was often the object of ecclesiastical discipline. Yet members of Paris developed the theory of conciliar government of the church at the time of the schism, while fourteenth-century Oxford, the home of the philosopher William of Ockham (Occam) and of John Wyclif, opened up lines of speculation that were opposed by orthodox thinking. In theory Oxford was subject to the discipline of the large and unwieldy diocese of Lincoln, whose distant bishop, although chancellor of the university, often found it difficult to exert his authority. His seal (53) shows him presiding over the students. Picture 54 shows Chaucer's Clerk of Oxford carrying a clasp-bound vellum book.

As literacy became more general among the laity (55) and the secular authority began to

53

54

55

56

found universities, it became impossible to enforce a religious monopoly of thought. The invention of printing with moveable type (58) from the 1460's produced a flood of books that soon included a growing number of "heretical" works. In Italy, the womb of the Renaissance, students and scholars (56) began to challenge old ideas. Literacy produced questions on all hands, and the church, one of the great bastions of the medieval establish-ment, began to look to its security. The new spirit of inquiry was also dramatically encouraged by the newly acquired learning from the Arab world, where many Greek works unknown to the West had long been studied.

In picture (59) a thirteenth-century French astronomer uses an Arab astrolabe, an instrument employed in England from about 1280 (57). Greek geometrical instruments (60) also returned to use in this period.

57

58

59

60

CHAPTER TWO

LORDS AND KINGS

MEDIEVAL LAY SOCIETY was a hierarchy in which power and social position were determined by landholding. In its turn, landholding carried obligations of military service. At the head of the system was the monarch, the fount of privilege and, in theory, the mainspring of authority in the state. Potentially the monarchy was always the strongest institution in medieval politics. The degree to which its potentialities were realized, however, was determined by a wide variety of historical circumstances. In the ninth century, for a brief and breathtaking generation, the whole of continental Europe west of the Oder River and south of Scandinavia acknowledged the lordship of the Emperor Charlemagne. After his death this vast domain was broken up into three kingdoms by his sons, and it was these that the states of the late Middle Ages crystallized. Thanks to Charlemagne's conquests and the steady progress of missionary activity and commercial enterprise eastward, the lands of central Europe were brought into the family of Christendom. At the death of the German Emperor Frederick II the lands of the empire were flanked on the east by the Christian states of Hungary and Poland. In both these states the monarchy was to enjoy a few generations of power and prestige, but only at the expense of heavy concessions to the great families of the landowning aristocracy. By the end of the Middle Ages, these had held their privileged position against royal encroachments so successfully that the kingdom of Poland broke up of its own accord into a group of estates whose owners were virtual sovereigns, while Hungary fell easy prey to the Turks in the sixteenth century.

A similar fate befell even the great might of the Empire, which under Frederick II had extended its way throughout the peninsula of Italy. The sheer size of the empire was too great for the resources of medieval monarchy, although the eleventh- and twelfth-century emperors had made heroic attempts to handle the problems. But there were many divisive influences that would have tended to shatter the empire even if the problems of geography had been overcome. In northern Italy the exploding commercial power of the cities made them more than a match even for Frederick Barbarossa himself. To the north of the Alps history played a crucial and damaging role. Territories such as the duchy of Bavaria or Saxony and the kingdom of Bohemia were large blocks of territory with long traditions of identity and pride in a pre-Christian past. Their traditions of independence were held in check during the reigns of the strong emperors but revived to help the breakup of the empire during the later Middle Ages.

The kings of France and the Iberian monarchs of Aragon, Navarre, Leon and Castile also had severe but different problems. The monarchs of the Spanish peninsula, which in the mid-twelfth century had added Portugal to their ranks, were engrossed in their struggle to push back the power of the Arab caliphates created during the eighth century. In France the monarchy founded by the Capetian house A.D. 940 hung onto the trappings of power without its reality for some two centuries before it was able to make real headway against its powerful vassals. The problem was that although the territorial magnates recognized the ultimate supremacy of the monarch from whom they derived the title to their land, the king's real power depended on the estates personally owned by the royal house. By degrees these were extended, but even in the thirteenth century they constituted only a small band of territory based on Paris and Bourges about 150 miles to the south. The duchy of Normandy, although a fief of the French crown, was in the domain of the King of England; the duchy of Brittany rejected outright the claims of Paris; in the south the powerful dukes of Aquitaine (also the kings of England) and the counts of Toulouse also fought to maintain their independence of the French crown.

But the French kings had certain advantages. They controlled Paris; the fact that large tracts of their kingdom acknowledged their supremacy, even if only in theory, proved to be of great importance as those claims gained strength simply by remaining uncontested; finally, by a remarkable genetic character, the kings of the House of Capet were able to provide an unbroken line of male heirs over the astonishing period of three and a half centuries. By the time the direct line finally died out in 1320, the idea of an elective monarchy was dead beyond recall. The French royal house was able to withstand more than a century of punishing war against English claims.

The basic problem for the rulers of the empire was that the traditional idea of elective kingship, derived from an ancient Teutonic past, remained vital. While the aristocratic dynasties could hand down their lands from father to son, the choice of emperor fell time and again into the hands of the princes who naturally made it their business to elect a member of a weak house. In England the principle of an elective kingship had been firmly rejected by its Norman conqueror, William. As a result, England soon boasted the most powerful and centralized monarchy in Europe. The barons knew who they must thank for their new territories, so that from the first the position of the crown as head of the lay establishment was clear in practice and in theory. But William made a crucial and typically farsighted move in the way he distributed the spoils of conquest among his followers. Learning from the situation in France and the powerful earldom in England before his invasion, he handed out the conquered lands in small scattered holdings.

The tension between the king and his great lords that remained part of the fabric of European society in the Middle Ages and beyond derived from these events. But the authority of the monarchy was slowly consolidated, and the lay establishment began to develop the same kind of solidarity as the church. No king could hope to rule for long against the wishes of his most powerful subjects. For the mass of the population, lacking privileges of birth or wealth, the emergence of a strong royal power was an advantage. But the process was a long one, and the nobility retained its position as a class throughout the Middle Ages.

The paintings reproduced on these pages are a vivid record of the power and magnificence of medieval monarchy. Crowned and anointed by the greatest bishops in the land (62, 65), constantly pressed by courtiers and petitioners (63), or visiting his scattered castles (64), the great prince might still sometimes share the cares of state with his fool (61). At the head of the state stood the king and, where the hereditary principle was firmly entrenched, this could mean a child monarch. By a quirk of fate both England and France had child monarchs during the 1370's and 1380's and were ruled by regency councils acting on behalf of the boy kings Richard II and Charles VI. Since monarchy depended ultimately on the qualities of one man, it was always a severe weakness of the system; a child king was a great test for any medieval state. Charles VI's frequent mental illnesses,

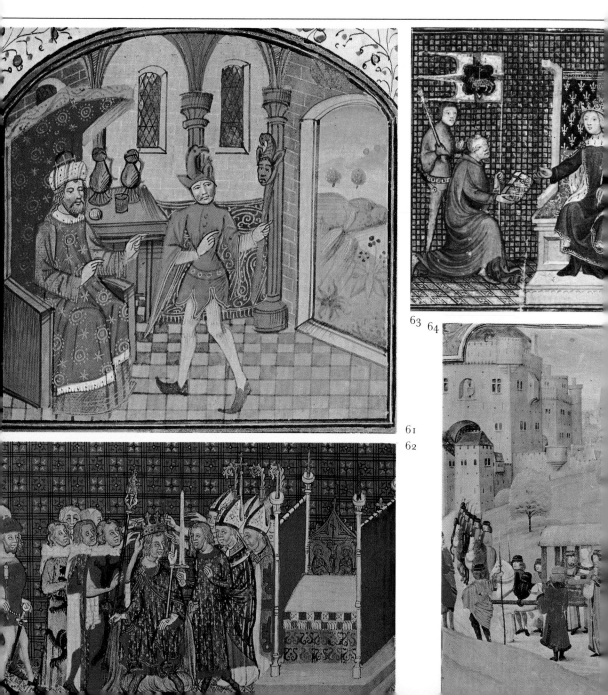

63 64

61
62

too, lay France open to the predatory ambitions of the king's uncles. In England the king was not mad but showed an uncomfortable tendency toward real authority. He paid for his presumption with deposition and death, despite his anointment with holy oil.

Theories of kingship had changed since the eleventh century, when some theorists had allowed the monarch the status of Christ's vicar in his kingdom. At this early period, too,

Edward the Confessor of England and Robert the Pious of France were held to have the power of healing by virtue of their office, and their monarchies, weak in secular terms, enjoyed a growing aura of sanctity. By the time of Richard II the kings of England had risen to a position of undisputed political strength, and their reputation for otherworldliness was small. This picture (66) shows a great prince at table.

65

66

The coronation was a solemn ceremonial, potent with symbolism and giving the king a claim on the respect and obedience of his subjects that no other great man in the land could equal. The coronation of the boy King Richard in 1377, had been stage-managed by his uncle John of Gaunt to buttress the reputation of the monarchy and the royal family at a time when it had been somewhat tarnished by the senile decline of the once-famous King Edward III. As steward of England, Gaunt supervised the arrangements both for the magnificent procession and for the coronation service. Even in England the memory of an elective monarchy survived. Before the king took the oath, the people were asked for their will and consent to his inauguration; at the coronation of Richard II, the question was put after the oath so that the answer became merely the voice of popular acclaim. In both

English and French (67) coronations of the time, the crowning was followed by a solemn act of dedication by the lay and religious magnates in which they touched the crown. Such a gesture might carry undesirable implications, as if the great men claimed a part in the making of the king and a share in his prerogatives. To guard against this, John of Gaunt arranged that this traditional gesture should simply denote the bishops' and nobles' pledge to share in the burdens of office. Kings, like all lords, were expected to dispense largess (69), but it was in his power to grant benefits and confer power on the greatest in the land. Picture 68 shows the king presiding over his supreme court while an usher copies down a new decree. In (70) and (71) we see both nobility and humble folk pressing petitions on the king. Figure (70) is from a manuscript of Froissart's *Chronicles*.

71

70

34 The peace of Christendom revolved around the amity of its kings. Picture 76 shows Edward III of England paying homage to Philip IV of France for the duchy of Aquitaine. At all times, kings were eternally pressed with advice, demands, and petitions. Even the greatest noble would not disdain to attempt to gain the ear of a powerful king, and to lose royal support could mean the destruction of a career.

Such were the potentialities of medieval kingship at its fullest. But the history of Europe shows that despite the prestige and respect enjoyed by strong kings, their weaker colleagues could expect little mercy if they lost control of their great men. The pomp and semimystical ceremony of his coronation could not save Richard from the ambition of his cousin Henry of Bolingbroke, who in 1399 "persuaded" him to abdicate and himself

72

73 75

took the crown basing his claim on the novel idea of parliamentary acclaim. German princes of the empire were actually able to determine the succession on certain occasions. In France the most powerful nobles were able, in the reign of a weak king, either to ignore the crown or to control it for their own ends. In England, where the hereditary succession had not flowed so smoothly and the respect for the royal house was not so ingrained, the throne was five times usurped between 1200 and 1500. In feudal terms the king, although lord over all (72), was expected to abide by the requirements of "good lordship." A breach in this "feudal contract" might well justify rebellion. In the Middle Ages, as in later times, strong men have never had to look far for pretexts to disobey the law. In pictures 74, 75, 76, 77 we see kings feasting and entertaining their nobles.

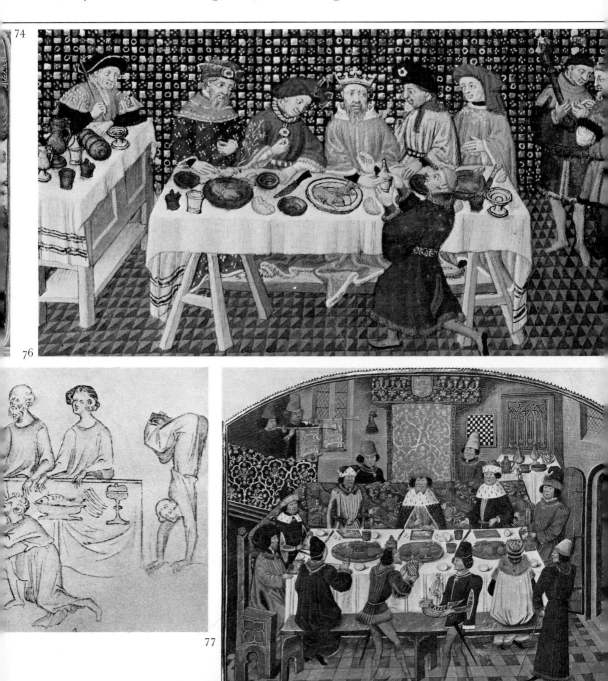

74

76

77

The court was inevitably the focus of political activity in any state with a reasonably flourishing monarch. Since it was the seat of power, it usually also became the focus of fashionable social life. In the mid-fourteenth century, when the king was at the height of his powers, the court of Edward III of England became a model for Europe, and it was there that the immensely popular cult of polite chivalry gained its greatest champion. Later the lead

was to be taken by the dukes of Burgundy, whose ambition to become kings led them to don the trappings of kingship. In the magnificence of their feasts (78), the elaborate nature of the ceremonial at their court (80), and the brilliance of dress and display by their courtiers they outshone every royal court in Europe. Burgundy thrived largely from the shameless plunder of the royal coffers by the dukes during the reign of Charles VI, when

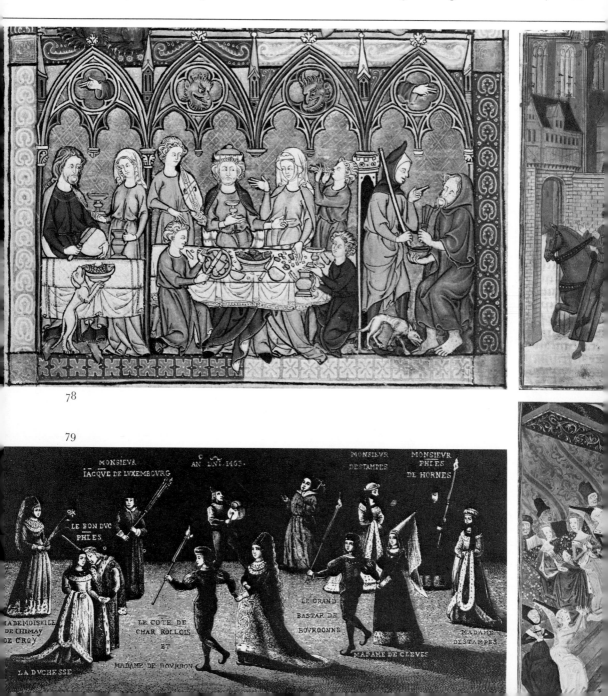

78

79

they were from time to time, the king's "advisers." During this period (the late fourteenth century) the French court was still brilliant, and its balls and state dances (79) were already well known. The most famous of all was the ill-fated *bal des ardentes* (81)—a costume dance at which several young courtiers, disguised as wild men or savages, were accidentally burned to death.

Feasting, ceremonial, and, above all, danc-ing were the chief diversions in the halls of medieval Europe. Here is a torchlight dance in the court of Burgundy in 1463 (79). Most of the stately court dances were derived from boisterous, not to say crude, folk dances. Even the instruments used to accompany noble and peasant were the same, the folk combination of pipe and tabor long remaining popular at lordly feasts like this Christmastide in Nuremberg in 1493 (82).

37

82

80

81 83

Despite the elegance of his manners and the luxury of his house and dress, the medieval noble and courtier retained much of the "robber baron" blood of his ancestors who had founded aristocratic Europe. The classic division of roles in the medieval world was between the men who prayed, those who worked in the fields to provide food, and those who carried arms to protect the community. This idea had been first stated by Alfred the Great of England, in a century when civilization itself seemed threatened by the depredations of the Norsemen. But in a later age, when Christian kings and princes rivaled one another in war, the prime function to the aristocracy remained that of warfare. Physical combat in any form was a delight.

This found expression in times of peace in the tournament arising in the later twelfth century. It remained for a long time a com-

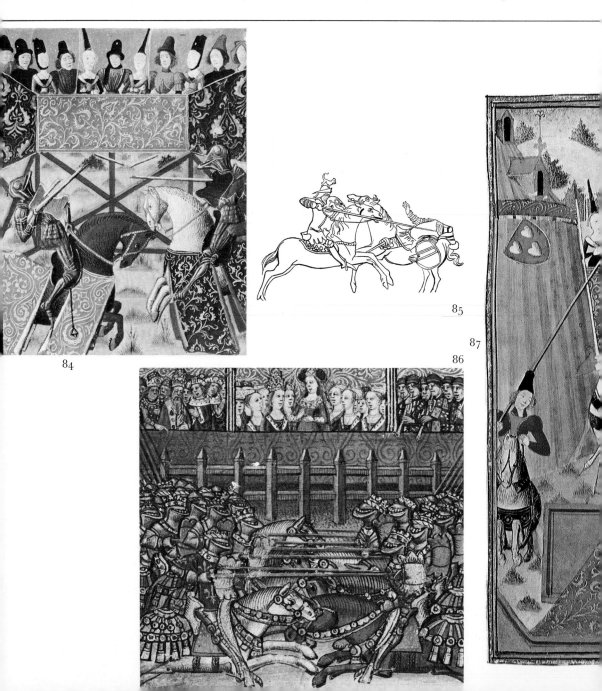

84

85

86

87

radely but bloody conflict (86). It differed from actual war only because no political or territorial issue divided the combatants. But men were often killed, ransoms were exacted and armour was taken as a prize of victory. In such *melées* humble knights who were good swordsmen could, and did, make their fortune and found a dynasty. But increasingly, kings came to control this rowdy and socially disruptive free-for-all, and from the thirteenth century onward the tournament became subject to increasingly stringent regulations, watched over by the king (84). The regulations concerned the issue of challenges, the arming of the knights, and the many other aspects of the combat. In earlier times a tournament had often consisted of a battle between rival "armies" of a hundred knights or more. Later personal combat (85) often under ritual supervision was more common (87).

40 For the nobleman the dividing line between the mock battles of the tournament and the realities of war was blurred. The panoply of feasting and comradeship was the same in both (89). In neither case did the gentleman expect to meet his death—unless by the unmannerly hands of a foot soldier when he had fallen or by the deadly storm of arrows of the bowmen. Pride, chivalry, and profit alike prompted his victor to save his life for the rich ransom that could be expected. Even on crusade the Christian knight, if he survived the first encounter, need not fear for his life or liberty. At the crushing defeat of Nicopolis (Emmaus) in 1396 the leader of the expedition, John, heir of Philip the Bold of Burgundy, won a European reputation for his courage and the soubriquet "the Fearless." He was captured but returned home a few months later, once a huge ransom had been paid into

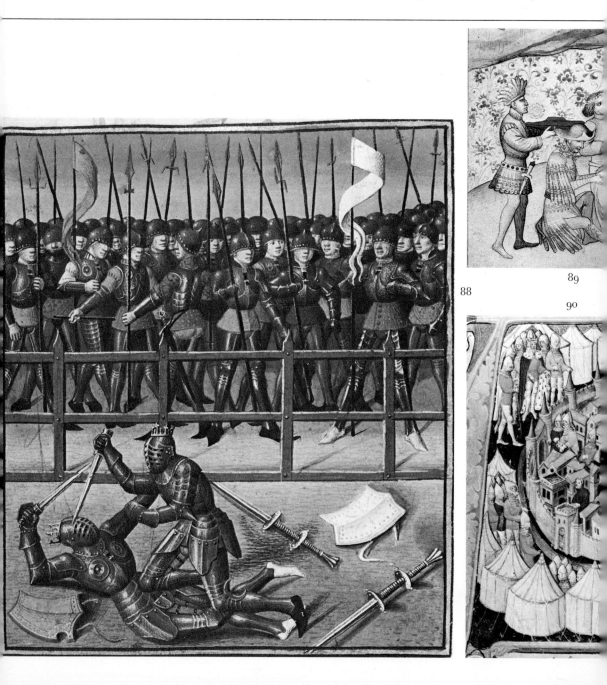

88

89

90

the coffers of the sultan (91). He had led the armies of Christendom to massive defeat.

Medieval kings and princes are said on occasion to have made fine gestures of settling their disputes in private combat, but such encounters happened only in the pages of romance (88).

A chronicler called the siege of Neuss, in the 1470's, the finest school of chivalry in Europe. He described the fields around the town covered with the gaily adorned pavilions and tents of the knights and said that many who had to come to the war in support of the Duke of Burgundy were really there to enjoy the tournaments and delights of camp life with the most splendid of Europe's rulers. Merchants and tradesmen of all kinds had been brought with the besieging army so that the town under siege seemed to be surrounded by a second town (90).

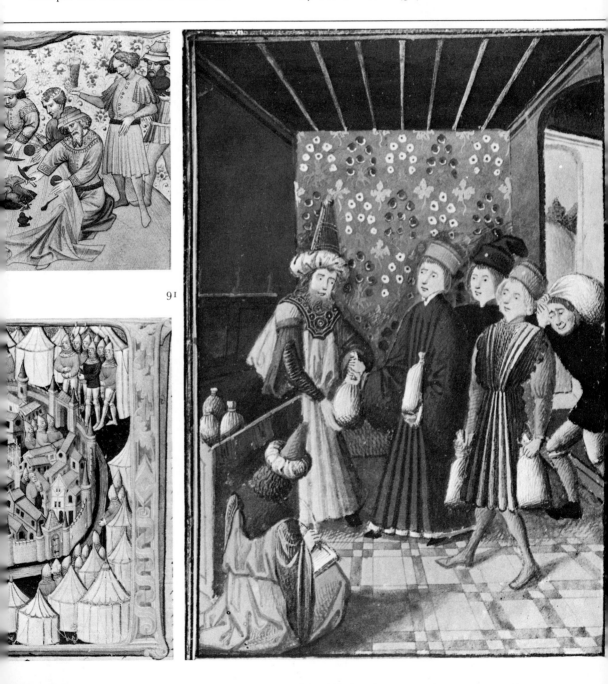

91

Warfare was as bestial in the Middle Ages as it is today. Hand-to-hand combat, whether on sea or land, was a bloody business, and many a fine city fell to the mercies of a brutal soldiery (92, 93). If the "good old days" ever existed, it was certainly not in the period we are studying in this book, when every large town had to be strongly fortified (94), and even church dignitaries were forced to submit to the sword (95). Recent research, however, has suggested that the term "the laws of war" was more than an empty turn of phrase. Conventions were followed about the surrender of towns, the capture of prisoners, and many other aspects of warfare that went some way to reducing the horrors of pillage and arson that fell in the wake of a medieval army. But the legalistic code seldom benefited civilian by-

92

93

94

96

standers. Nevertheless, the profession of arms was considered a noble one, and for the young blood, a campaign was an event of high excitement and offered the chance to mark his entry into the ranks of knighthood with some heroic deed (96, 97). The cult of knighthood had arisen during the twelfth century. The simple aggressive instincts of Europe's fighting class received a veneer of civilization from the church and from the poetic cult of courtly love that sprang up in the domains of the Count of Toulouse and around the figure of the beautiful and imperious Eleanor of Aquitaine. By the fourteenth century the concept had achieved a classic synthesis: The urge of the fighting man was united with the sense of a Christian duty to defend the weak and with the ideal of protecting the weaker sex.

95

97

44 The chivalric code of love elevated love to the plane of an almost religious game (98, 99, 100). Marriage remained a matter of dynastic politics, as in the marriage between the Duke of Burgundy and the daughter of the Count of Flanders (101). In the high period of the courtly epic the great ladies in attendance to Queen Eleanor held real courts of love with rules of procedure that aped those of legal justice (102). The Castle of Love under attack was treated in story and legend as though an episode in siege warfare (103). And in reality the ladies of the house often did the arming of their lord (104).

As the Middle Ages progressed, warfare became an increasingly professional business, and the noble pursuit of arms became a means of earning a living. It was often highly profitable. Knighthood became a glamorous and mystical fraternity in which kings, noble-

98

99

100

101

men, and gentlemen enjoyed a kind of equality within the rules of the order. Since the twelfth century, the semilegendary King Arthur had been the paragon of virtue for the Christian knight. It was probably a conscious act of statecraft, which well expressed his own personal predilections, that led King Edward III to found the noble Order of the Garter, which is still a high award today in Britain. With its blend of military prowess and courtly deference to the lady this was the first formal order of chivalry. The hard facts of politics and war changed little, but the members of the lay establishment welcomed an institution that bound them to their sovereign in new and intimate ties of allegiance and that lent a new dignity and elegance to their urge for display. This type of courtly confraternity reinforced the weakening ties of feudal obligation with a new bond—the gentleman's code.

102

103

104

The rulers of the medieval world were not play actors. The displays of chivalry (105) and courtly love (106, 108) were more vivid but no less real to their devotees than the lip service that the modern world pays to "business ethics" and "democratic processes." The great men of the Middle Ages recognized the existence of higher principles of life than the self-interested greed that so often governed their daily conduct. Like all members of all sophisticated civilizations, they read their own values into the world of the past. The medieval knight revered the great deeds of the ancient Romans for what he regarded as their chivalric

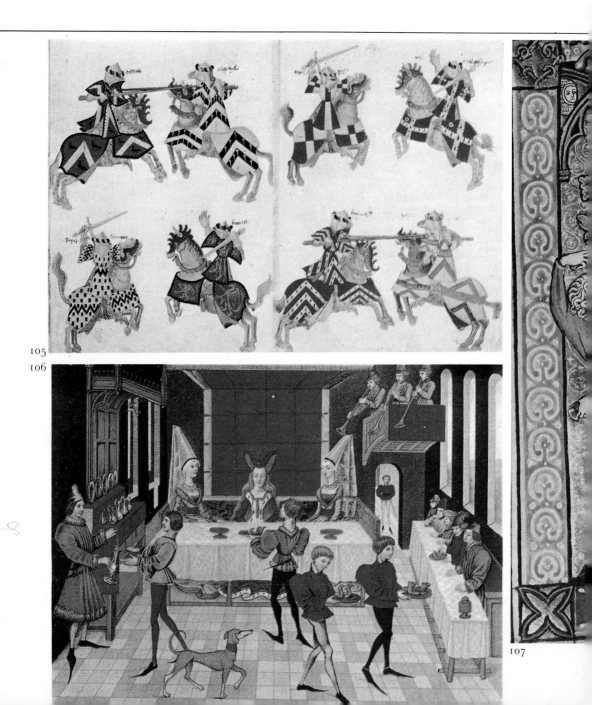

105
106

107

prowess. Seeking a respectable Christian patron, he endowed the shadowy figure of St. George (109) with the virtues of the Christian knight, while Goliath was portrayed as an evil knight (107). Even the princes of Renaissance Italy were devotees of this northern cult, which numbered Alexander the Great and King Arthur among its worthies, and the sense of living in an age-old tradition was an important bond between the ruling classes of Christian Europe.

108

109

48 The knight traditionally fought on horseback, and indeed many a king and prince virtually lived in the saddle. Travel was by horse, and the greatest diversion of monarchs and their aristocracy was the hunt, the "sport of kings" (110). The art of the breeder had produced several specialized types of horse. These ranged from the heavy war-horse, or *destrier*, capable of carrying a man fully armed in steel at a gallop, to the lighter hunter from which modern breeds are descended. Horses were among the most valuable of the rich presents that regularly changed hands between nobles and rulers. The mysteries of the hunt were served by a large establishment of skilled men to tend the horses, train and care for the hunting dogs (111), and supervise the ritual of chase (112). The repertoire of horn calls (115) still heard in the hunting field were developed during the Middle Ages and must

110

111

112

have been the most familiar music in the ears of many a nobleman and his lady. In picture (113) the hunters are resting for food.

A great hunting establishment was also equipped with a mews. Indeed the passion for falconry or hawking was second only to the chase. Figure (114) first illustrated a French hunting book of the fourteenth century. The techniques were even more complicated, and the training of the birds was regarded as a high mystery. Like so much else in medieval life, falconry was subject to strict rules designed to protect the status of the members of the social hierarchy. Only kings were permitted the use of the great gyrfalcon; nobles had to hunt with peregrines and priests and monks with the sparrow hawk. Falconry was one of the great medieval arts; among its devotees perhaps the greatest was the Emperor Frederick II whose treatise remains a classic.

114

113

115

50 The social order, loosely termed feudalism, had finally emerged in Europe in the ninth and tenth centuries. At that time, the ravages of Vikings, Magyars, and Saracens had forced the small man to seek protection from his more powerful co-dwellers and had forced the ruler to rely on the help of his great men. At the heart of these arrangements lay what Jean Jacques Rousseau might have called a social contract. Freeholds were surrendered and authority was conferred in return for military protection. In succeeding centuries, war—the main occupation of the noble class— became a ruling passion, and was fought with weapons of growing sophistication (119). Yet the basic idea that wealth and power carry obligations remained, reinforced by the Christian ethic. The rich, for example, had a duty to beggars (116, 117). Men's actions often belie their beliefs, but those beliefs are always

116

117

118

illuminating when we seek to understand a different age. In our generation we accept that every man has the right to power and wealth if he can earn it. The profit motive is part of modern society. Medieval man evolved a social code which, though often disregarded, meant that wealth and power were a trust demanding generosity and regard toward those less fortunate.

The life of the king or the noble was one of privilege and luxury (120). His wealth derived from the land and was lavishly spent on pleasure palaces, delightful gardens, expensive amusements, feasts, and clothes. Another sign of grandeur was patronage on a massive scale (118). Artists and writers, once largely in the service of the church, gradually came to rely on commissions from the nobility. The poor and members of the household could expect largess and alms when the great went abroad.

119   120

Within the walled garden of his town house (121), receiving petitioners or dispensing justice in his hall (122), and finally laid to rest in an imposing monument in the great church of his district, the nobleman seemed an imposing figure. Figure (123) shows two such English monuments, dedicated to English knights. That on the left was built in 1327 to the memory of Sir John D'Aubernoun in Surrey, and that on the right, dated 1354, commemorates Sir John de Cobham in Kent. He lived remote from the hurly-burly of the life of his less fortunate fellows. Everything in his society was designed to emphasize his exalted rank. The rules of etiquette and precedence were extensive and meticulously observed. Days could be spent on deciding the correct mode of approach and salutation at the meeting of two great men. The seal of authority was used by lords, as well as kings.

121

122

The seal in figure (124) belonged to Robert Fitzwalter, an English baron. Laws were passed attempting to regulate the clothes worn by the various classes of society.

Yet the fall of great men from power was a common enough event. Members of the lesser nobility, who were content to remain on their estates, could look forward to a relatively untroubled enjoyment of their wealth and possessions. But the more ambitious ran the risks of disgrace, even death. In the year 1407 the young Duke of Orléans, a friend of Charles the Dauphin, was done to death in the streets of Paris by the agents of John the Fearless of Burgundy. The rivalry between the dauphin and Burgundy poisoned French public life and at the hoped-for reconciliation between the two parties twelve years later, Duke John was murdered, in his turn, in the presence of the dauphin.

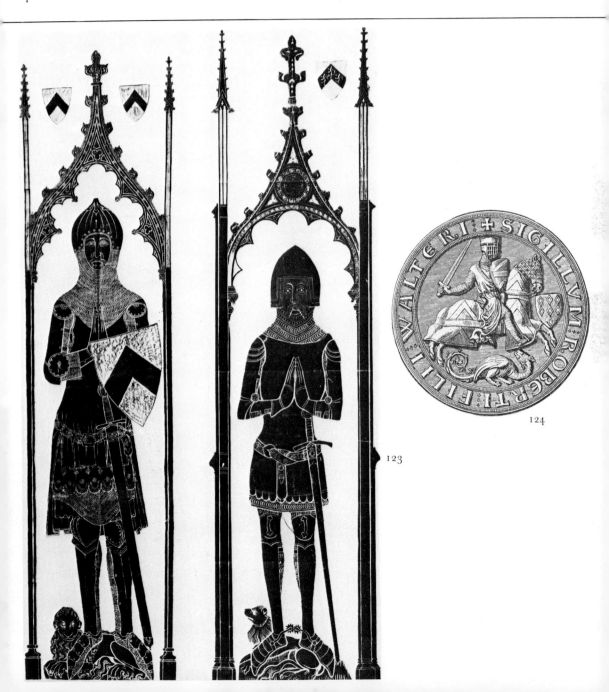

123

124

54 The position of women in the Middle Ages was, in theory, one of utter subjection. In practice, however, they might enjoy great influence. Wives were supposed to give obedience to their husbands, but unmarried women were not allowed to go out without chaperones, while widows were often obliged to return to their parents' houses where convention gave them a lower status than their unmarried sisters. But in most ranks of society, women, particularly married women, exercised complete authority within their households. Often they needed real administrative ability if they were to supervise a numerous staff and a large establishment. In the upper ranks of society, women (125, 127) were frequently very powerful and could enjoy all the good things of life, such as their own entertainment (129), and travels around the countryside (128). During the earlier Middle Ages a lord might well

125

126

127

128

leave his castle in the charge of his wife while he went to fight in the king's wars or on a crusade, and there are cases of a garrison under siege being commanded by the lady castellan. Some women such as St. Elizabeth of Hungary won reputations by their piety; others, such as Queen Matilda or Queen Eleanor of England, showed themselves equal to acting in the political world.

Perhaps the most important part played by women in European cultural history was in marriage itself. Not only did high marriages have important political objectives, but the princess or heiress would bring to her husband's court an entourage (126) of her countrymen and with them the cultural traditions of a distant part of the world. In such journeys and unions we can see the very arteries that carried the lifeblood of cultural influence and helped the spread of new ideas.

129

The lady and her lap dog (134) were a common enough sight in polite medieval society. Ladies often joined their lords in the hunting field and sometimes indulged in the pleasure of gaming. Dice and many types of board games were common in all ranks of society and were often played for stakes. Although gaming was not so peculiarly the vice of the idle rich as it was to become in the eighteenth and nineteenth centuries, it was common enough. Games of all types were pressed into service. Among the most popular were games of dice (130, 131, 133) and backgammon (132), which combines the throw of the dice with a large element of skill. With the introduction of chess in the early twelfth century the nobility of Europe had a new and enthralling pastime and one that, like most other games played for money, could lead to angry words and even to blows. Figures (135)

130

132

131

133

and (136) show French noblewomen at the chess board, and figure (137) pictures soldiers playing chess during a military campaign.

A contemporary chronicler describes a game between the Black Prince and Philip, son of John II of France (the latter had been imprisoned in England since his capture on the field of Poitiers): "One day a dispute arose over a knight that had been taken. One said it was a fair move while the other claimed it was false. As often happens in this game, where even the wisest get impatient, hot words followed. Indeed both sprang to their feet in anger, reaching for their poignards and spoiling for a fight . . . and all on account of a trifling piece of wood or ivory carved in the likeness of a knight." Fortunately, the day was saved by a group of English courtiers who gallantly admitted the justice of the prisoner's claim against the prince.

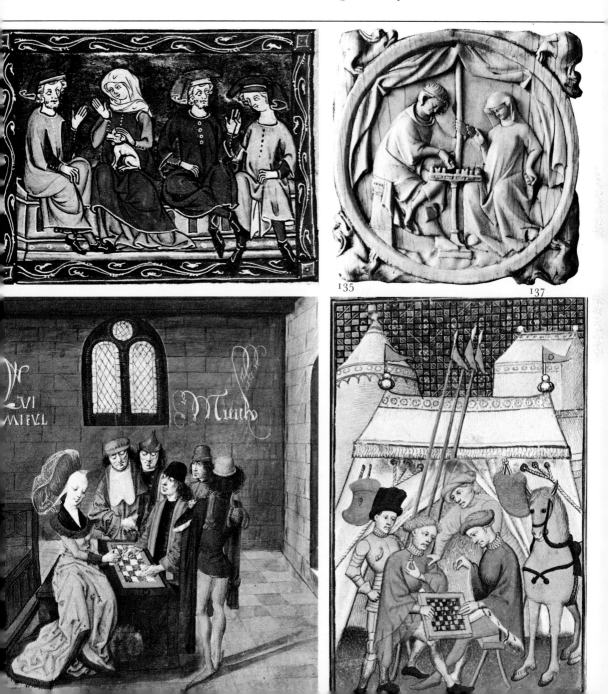

135

137

In 1500 the nobility of Europe, if not actually in decline, found their position and their class eroded. The towns had become firmly entrenched and had thrown up a new kind of rich man to join the ranks of the lay establishment—the merchant. Furthermore, by the end of the fifteenth century the central power had established itself very strongly in the western monarchies and in the larger principates of the German empire. As a class, of course, the nobles were still the king's wealthiest and most powerful subjects. Many among the more enlightened of them had been studying the agricultural potential of their vast holdings to make them more profitable (138, 139, 142).

Between the years 1200 and 1500 a significant and far-reaching change took place in social attitudes, perhaps summed up as "domestication." Around 1200 the life of the

138

139

140

141

great was still a very public affair. Great private houses as such barely existed. The lord and his household were frequently on the move between his various castles and fortified residences, as was the king himself. Even the most magnificent castle had few private rooms. By the late fifteenth century, however, possibly after the example of the comfortable town houses of the merchants, castles and palaces had the richest possible accommodations—sizeable kitchens, guest rooms, and chambers of all kinds under the same roof. This new interest in domestic comfort included a desire to improve the amenities of the surrounding lands (143). Books on estate management were carefully copied out by hand, advising not only on the principles of husbandry (140, 141), but also on the best ways to lay out gardens and pleasure grounds (144).

142

143

144

CHAPTER THREE

THE RISE OF TOWNS AND MERCHANTS

BY 1500 THE MERCHANT CLASS had for more than 100 years been a leading member of the medieval power structure. But before discussing this emergence, a special feature of the period, we must examine the situation in Europe as a whole, for there were wide divergencies in the rate of development from one region to another.

It is to Italy that we must first turn. Although, like the rest of Europe, Italy had been ravaged and disrupted by the barbarian invasions of the fifth century, her cities had never entirely lost touch with the urban tradition of their Roman past. There, in the old home of the Roman Empire, that tradition was already 1,000 years old. The administrative system of the classical world had, in fact, given place to that of Theodoric the Ostrogoth, but much continuity had been preserved. During the following centuries Italian society, like that elsewhere, had a military aristocracy imposed on it, based on feudal landholding. However, this class never struck such deep roots as it did north of the Alps. From the tenth century, it began to feel the impact of new and typically Italian developments. The processes of trade were reviving throughout Europe most vigorously in the towns of Italy which had constant trading with the urban civilization of the eastern Mediterranean, represented by the Byzantine Empire, the heir to Rome. Thanks partly to a population explosion that gathered strength through the tenth and eleventh centuries, northern Europe entered a new era of wealth. The demand for the luxury goods of the East increased.

The trade lanes from Constantinople to the north were thronged with more and more merchants as the years passed. The route up the Russian river system to the Baltic provided the wealth on which Kiev and Novgorod were founded, but the heaviest traffic lay along the Adriatic to the plain of the Po River and thence over the Alps. Towns like Pavia became busy entrepôts; merchants from the north brought caravans laden with woolen and linen cloths, weapons, horses, slaves and hunting dogs to barter with their colleagues from the south. The Italians who served the southern trade brought cargoes of fine jewelry, ivory, and, above all, spices to offer in exchange. Later silk, too, became an important product. Even at this stage, when the merchant venture often seemed like a heroic epic, a new class of professionals was growing up, based on such towns as Pavia, Venice, and Constantinople. The business of this new class depended on its expert knowledge of prices and exchange rates. Dominating this great artery of trade, Venice emerged as the first of a new type of commercial state that was soon to rule the Italian scene. From the tenth century on, Venice was a true merchant oligarchy. It was ruled by an elective head of state and government drawn from the leading families of the city. Other towns in Italy were to suffer generations of conflict between the landed aristocracy, heirs to the feudal past, the merchants, and the *popolo minuto*, the "little people." The latter were represented by the lesser guildsmen and the artisans employed by the various industries, chief among them the weavers of Florence. In each town the struggle took on a different form, but the overall pattern of Italian history in the later Middle Ages is one of struggle by the new merchant families to win control of the government. The outcome was not always as they wished. In any case, by the end of the fifteenth century the "aristocracy" of bankers and big merchants was in most towns becoming more and more like that which it had displaced. What was the significance of this struggle for European history as a whole? The Italian cities, in making good their claims to independence both of the papal and the imperial power, had emerged as sovereign states. In terms of corporate wealth, they could challenge the greatest kings in Europe. Many monarchs north of the Alps were happy to raise loans from an Italian banker, and the brilliance of the courts of Renaissance Italy, built on the proceeds of trade, is legendary. The rise of the Italian towns had great cultural effects, but we should never forget the less romantic but equally valuable part that they played in founding a European system of banking and credit. In northern Europe where royal power was slowly to gain the ascendant, French and English towns never won the independence and influence of those of Italy. But they were important enough. Paris and London held the keys to their kingdom, and down through the centuries their kings were careful to grant them charters and privileges to keep the loyalty of the citizens. International trade was focused, during the thirteenth century, on the great regional fairs. These were held, for example, in Champagne in France. In England the annual fairs at Winchester and Boston were major events, serving the needs of international trade. In addition to the overland trade, immense activity took place on the international sea lanes. This activity made Bristol the second city of England, for example, and above all gave the German merchants of the Hanseatic League of north German towns effective control of Baltic trade and agencies in all the main towns of northern Europe.

Probably the greatest concentration of wealth in the north was to be found in the towns of Flanders. These towns produced a culture second in brilliance only to that of Italy. Like townsmen everywhere, they fought to throw off the authority of their aristocratic rulers, but despite the immense wealth of cities like Ghent, Bruges, and Ypres, the battle was hard fought. Under the rule of the dukes of Burgundy in the fifteenth century the oligarchs of the town may be said to have lost.

From Italy to England, from Spain to northern Germany, the period of 1200 to 1500 saw the rise of a new class of wealthy and powerful men. They built the structure of a new Europe to join the classic trinity of king, church, and nobles. In their dress and manners, the merchants came to ape the nobility and indeed often joined its ranks, while within the walls of the towns they might rival the power of many a great lord on his domain.

Even the greatest medieval towns, like late fifteenth-century Nuremberg (145) in Germany or like Paris, were small by modern standards. At the end of the Middle Ages the largest European towns were probably those of Italy. Yet it is doubtful whether even Venice had as many as 100,000 inhabitants. In northern Europe, even 50,000 people constituted a large city. From the outside, a walled city offered an exciting prospect. Rising behind the walls were the spires of its many churches and the towers of its great houses. Needing regular upkeep, the walls involved the citizens in great expense, and the land near the walls was sometimes charged with their upkeep. In times of peace, buildings spread out beyond the circuit of the walls (149), but during an enemy campaign these humble dwellings were

145

146

147

148

liable to be destroyed in order to clear the approaches to the wall. As trade grew, so the merchants and the towns grew in importance; medieval rulers had to take more and more account of them. London had always held a central place in English politics so that after the suspicious death of Richard II in 1399, the usurper Henry IV took care that the late king's funeral should be conducted with all due pomp in the capital (146). In France the ancient city of Rheims—though it was not the capital— was also crucial since from time immemorial the kings of France had been crowned there. The coronation processions of kings (147) or the entry of members of the nobility into the town (150) were occasions of high ceremonial, and many an aristocrat visiting the rich houses of the patricians must have been impressed (148).

149

150

The leaders of the borough community, known collectively as the patricians, were often at odds with the princely rulers who tried to enforce ancient claims to suzerainty. It was patrician wealth that adorned the cities with handsome churches (154) and patrician interests that managed the conduct of city life. More than one merchant family was able to graduate into the ranks of the nobility, and in the rich appointments of their houses and the opulence of their clothes (151, 153) such families proclaimed their wealth and grandeur. Here is a richly dressed French merchant, with fur cap (156). The Merchant from an early manuscript edition of Chaucer's *Canterbury Tales* is shown in picture 158. Inside their homes, everything was done to ensure comfort, although conditions outside were often

153

151

152

154

155

squalid and dangerous. The point is nicely summed up in a contemporary picture showing the harshness of winter contrasted with snug conditions by the fireside (155). But the medieval town dweller had more than the inclemencies of the weather to contend with. Medieval town sewage was notoriously bad. The overhanging upper stories of half-timbered houses shut out the daylight from the streets (152). At all times the hazards to health were matched by those to property and life. Robbery and violence on the streets were frequent, and housebreaking was commonplace. The source of the nobles' wealth lay in the fields and the toil of the peasant class, but the merchant had to store up his treasure in movables. Bolts, locks, and bars were an essential guard against night burglars (157).

156

157

158

The ornate façades of these German burghers' houses in Rothenburg (159) sum up for the outside world the wealth of its builder and the magnificence we may expect inside. At home, with his family, the worthy man expected to eat of the best and be well attended by his own servants (160, 161, 162). When he had company, a boisterous drinking party could sometimes get out of hand (163). As the guests abovestairs get down to the business of serious drinking, the red-nosed steward in the cellar, while ensuring the wine is running clear, is also giving it the benefit of a final tasting. Perhaps he and the guests are drinking the popular new brandywine.

Nor were the calmer pleasures of life forgotten. The medieval town was a congested huddle of buildings, magnificence, jostling

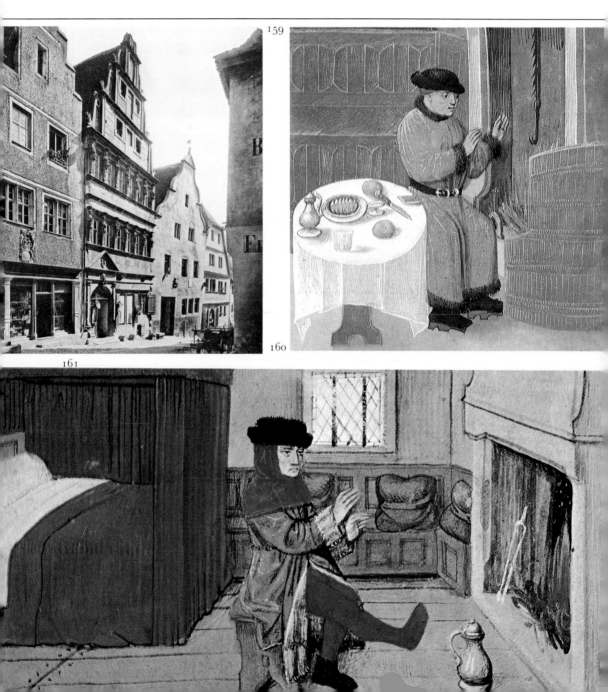

159

160

161

squalor, and great families living in the same apartment houses as the poorer members of society. There was no town planning as we understand it. The open fields were never far away. Here townsmen rich or poor, could take their sport (164), but for the businessman without the time or inclination to take a walk beyond the walls, the delights of having his own walled garden were indispensable (165).

Designed with care, these gardens became very popular. Diaries and daybooks lovingly record the purchase of plants for the garden and dwell on the pleasure the hardheaded merchant derived from a walk in his own green sanctuary. Here the cares of a troubled and changing world could for a moment be forgotten, and the wealthy man could pass his time in peace.

162

164

163

165

Waterborne trade played a far larger part in the trade of medieval Europe than it does today. The bad state of the roads encouraged full use of navigable river systems (166). Much cargo was also carried by coastal vessels, for example, the English sea coal brought from Newcastle to London. The comparatively small size of the medieval "cog" (coastal vessel) meant that it could dock in ports far upriver from the sea (169). This enabled Bristol, for example, to be among the most important towns in England. The most famous case, however, was Bruges. Now an inland town, it was in the fourteenth century the most important trading port in northern Europe. But its power declined as the river slowly silted up, despite desperate attempts by the city authorities to dredge the channel open. One of the most famous sights of the northern ports was the great crane at Bruges, worked

166

168

167

by a treadmill operated by four men. Other parts were equipped with similar gear, such as the crane in Antwerp docks illustrated in picture 167.

The small size and tublike shape of the medieval merchant vessel in northern waters is perfectly illustrated by scenes from a shipyard on an estuary (168) and the quay of the river port (171). These same ships were seized by the authorities to serve in time of war, with ramparts of castles built fore and aft (170). In the Mediterranean, untroubled by tides and rarely as stormy as the North Sea, longer and narrower craft were sometimes used. Italian galleys became a common sight, even as far north as Southampton and Bruges. Growing seaborne trade brought wealth and power to many towns, the most famous of which was Venice, built on the sea itself, and pictured below in a woodcut of 1486 (172).

169

170

171

172

The artisans and small tradesmen (179), who formed the base of town society, were ruled by the guilds and associations formed by their masters. These had grown up as early as the eleventh century, when the towns of northern Europe were still subject to the authority of the great lords on whose land they stood. The hazards of overland trade and the need for codes of practice in the new merchant communities had led their leading members to form associations. These associations administered commercial law, regulated trade practices, had rules of membership, and supervised the quality of work. The merchant guilds concerned themselves with matters which were often of little interest to the lord, who was usually happy to be assured of his revenue without becoming involved in technical disputes among his townsmen. Gradually, the guilds won complete autonomy of jurisdiction

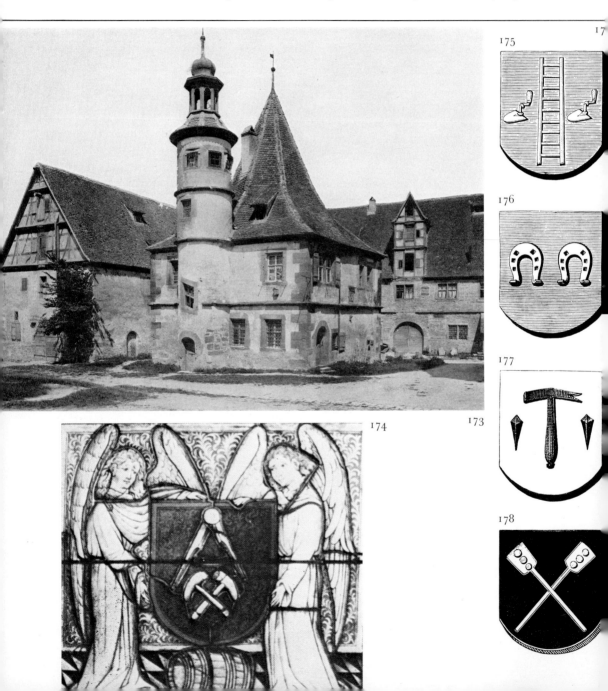

175

176

177

173

174

178

within the town boundaries. They became wealthy and powerful bodies, proud of their traditions, and united in a sense of common self-interest. They resisted the encroachments of aristocratic authority and those of the small masters and wage earners who made up the mass of the town population. At their height the guilds were the true masters of the towns of Europe, displaying their wealth in magnificent guild halls like this at Rothenburg (173),

and in badges and coats of arms proudly displayed at civic festivities and ceremonial. Illustrated are the coats of arms of a German cooper's guild (174), the Parisian slaters (175), the blacksmiths of St.-Lo in France (176), the Parisian nail makers (177), and the Parisian bankers (178). They were not unlike the heraldic shields of the peerage, which in a modest and practical way they perhaps sought to emulate.

Membership in a guild brought valuable commercial privileges and a position of power in the town to an individual. But it also carried obligations, both to the town and to other members of the confraternity. Designed to promote solidarity, the guilds worked hard to maintain it, and the solemn oaths sworn in council were strictly enforced. Guild members in Olmütz, Germany, taking an oath are shown in picture (182).

In a flourishing town like Rouen, all the major trades, such as the shoemakers (183) and carpenters, had their own guilds. In towns with a river trade, the lightermen (180) could be an especially important body. In certain cities, such as Milan and Augsburg, renowned widely for their fine armour, the armourers' guild would be of similar importance. So the specialties of the town's industry or trade were reflected in its government. Just as the guild

180

181

182

183

itself was managed by its most powerful members in the workshop, so the individual master claimed absolute authority over his apprentices (181). This is emphasized by the diminutive size of the apprentice as depicted in the picture of a fourteenth-century German armourer's shop (184). The authority of the masters of the guild was most in evidence when the apprentice came to complete a "masterpiece" under the watchful eyes of the guild's assessors.

In picture 185 French apprentice masons are making their masterpieces. In the later Middle Ages the guilds began to operate a closed shop, and this test was one way to control the number of independent masters. As the systems developed, more and more restrictive practices were evolved to maintain its old authority in the face of new economic circumstances. It gradually assisted in its own decline.

184

185

Depending on commerce for its life, the medieval town had many shops, but they were of a type unlike anything we know today. Picture 186 depicts a variety of tradesmen in the same street; in the background we can see a barber at work, and in the left foreground a tailor's shop. But this representation was more for the convenience of the artist than an accurate portrayal of any actual scene. The different trades tended to keep together in specific parts of the town. The clothiers' and upholsterers' quarter in fifteenth-century Bologna is shown in picture 189. No doubt this was because each trader wished to keep in close touch with activities of his rivals and to present his wares in direct competition. This

186

arrangement must have eased the task of the guildmasters, too, in supervising the lives of their members and guarding against the danger of nonguild members setting up unauthorized operations. The most obvious difference between medieval and modern premises is the absence of a display window. Food was usually sold from open stalls, like the English egg seller shown in this 1495 woodcut (188), or in covered markets, like the Italian fishmonger seen in 187. Some trades, however, came to use shops. In a scene in a Parisian butcher's shop (190) we can see the ever-present balance for weighing not only the goods but the money to pay for them, and the customer placing his order.

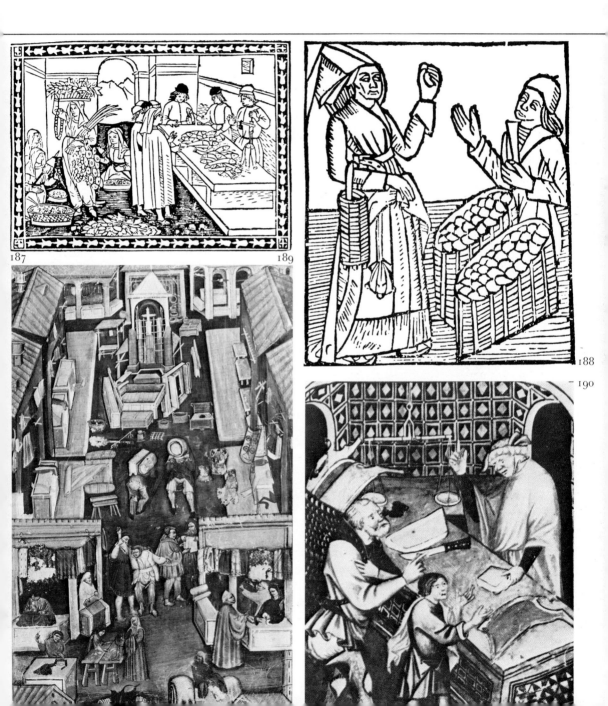

187

189

188

190

In the manufacturing trades, the shop and the workshop were often one and the same. In the higher class of shop frequented by rich patrons, such as jewelers (191, 192) the workroom might be in the rear part of the building. This enabled the gentry to make their selection free from the dirt and noise of the work. But even in these trades, such division between front and back shop was by no means usual. In other cases, such as at the French tailor (193) or the German shoemaker (194), the customer would expect to choose the cloth or leather from the shelves of the workroom while the masters' apprentices and journeymen were making up other orders. Customers often included passing pilgrims, such as the ones in a Flemish egg shop of 1486 shown in picture 195.

The aim of any medieval artisan or tradesman was to graduate to the position of an

191

192

193

independent master. This required capital, however, and many workers, after completing their apprenticeships, had to be content to earn wages working for someone else. Wages for apprentices were low but were supplemented with food and board. The compact establishment of a successful trader would consist of a workshop and a reception area for customers, with an apartment above for the proprietor and his family. At the top of the house would be small attic rooms for the apprentice and for the servants. The system, often one of thinly veiled exploitation, produced discontent and occasional riots in which the apprentices and journeymen tried to force improvements from their employers. Sometimes they brought mob violence onto the streets in protest against foreign traders in the town, who were stiffening the competition for the local men.

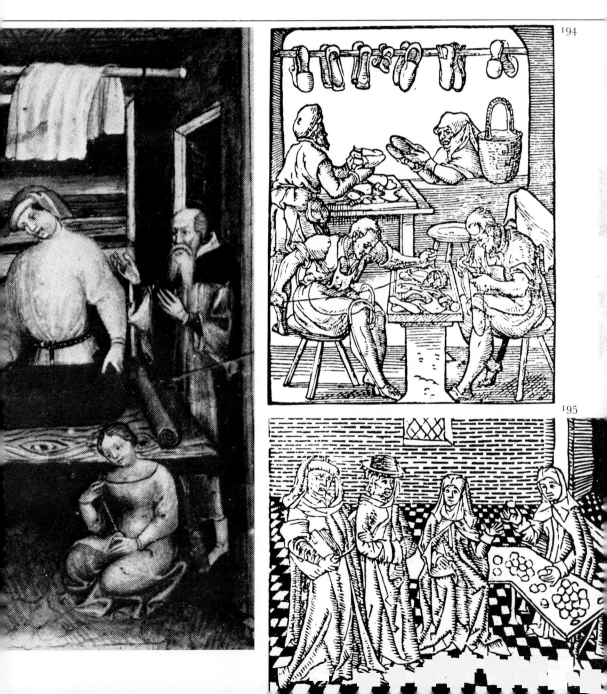

194

195

The medieval merchant and banker found himself in an anomalous position. It may be summed up in the famous motto of Francesco Dantini of Prato: "In the name of God and of profit." For despised by the aristocracy, he also came dangerously close to censure by the church, which powerfully condemned both usury and exorbitant profits. But the merchant's power and status naturally depended on the accumulation of profit and careful bookkeeping, as seen in an illustration from a medieval book for children on the four cardinal virtues (196). In the merchant's book, thrift and circumspection must have ranked high on the list. For if, looking to high profits and social advancements, he chose to lend to kings and princes, he had at that time no legal remedy if they chose to ignore their obliga-

196

tions. Perhaps the most famous instance was the crash of the Italian houses of Bardi and Peruzzi, bankers to King Edward III of England, who disclaimed his debts. In the fifteenth century the great Florentine house of Medici was careful to limit its lending to princes.

Avarice, represented by this fifteenth-century English merchant (197), was listed as one of the seven deadly sins. The church's con-demnation of usury must have made many a merchant approaching the end of a long and successful career fear for his immortal soul (198, 199). Indeed many of them wrote wills in which they made a general confession of all their faults, deliberate or otherwise, concerning the religious ban on usury. Treasure in heaven was no less important than treasure on earth.

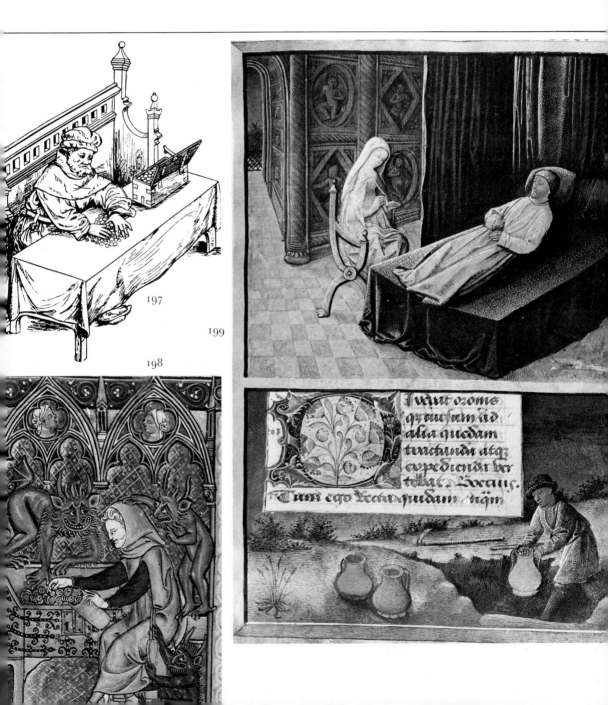

197

198

199

The use of money involved many problems. Large funds had to be physically transported from one distant town to another; the demand for risk capital grew as trade expanded. Ingenious minds set to work to find ways of operating that would stay within church law and force even the church to make use of bankers' services. The never-ending flow of revenue to Rome involved moving vast quantities of specie (200), and the security risks were, of course, enormous (203). As the merchant and banking community grew, it became possible by bills to make payments at one office on moneys received at another. Even the popes began to make use of this service.

The smooth operation of business rested basically on the soundness of the currencies in circulation. The gold and silver currency of England—like the silver groats of Henry VII (202) and gold florins and nobles of Edward

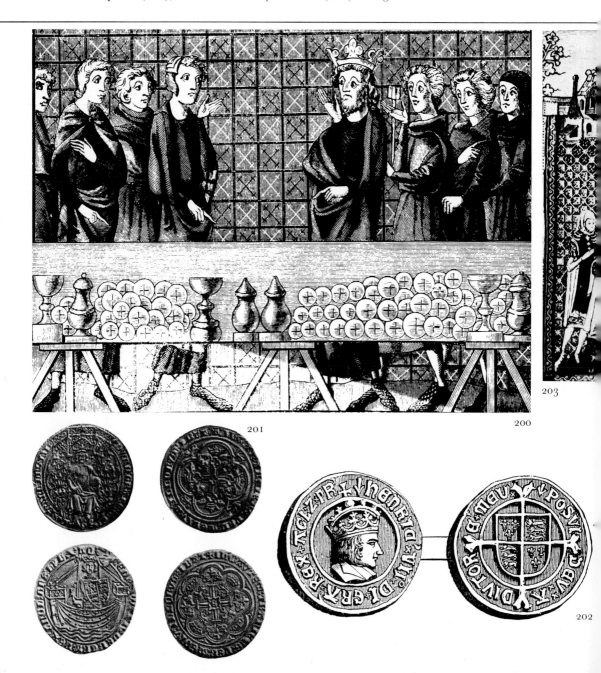

201

203

200

202

III (201)—were particularly prized. All states of any size and even important towns had the right to mint coins, and moneyers and assayers were skilled craftsmen (204). Strict penalties were imposed on counterfeiters. The scope for fraud (such as clipping) in the whole field of coinage, weights, and measures was immense. Scales were regularly used to check coins by weight, as shown in this stained glass window in Chartres Cathedral (205). Henry I of England was one of the first rulers to set up standards throughout his dominions; for a long time the different measures used from region to region were an open invitation to dishonesty. But in medieval terms, banking itself was in a sense fraudulent. Since the taking of outright interest was banned as usury, a standard time limit was set on the discounting of bills. Interest on a loan was thinly concealed as fluctuations in the exchange rates.

204

205

The skill, even audacity, of the medieval architect still causes astonishment today when we study the magnificent cathedrals and churches that survive throughout Europe. But there was much other building besides. The cathedrals of bishops and monks were matched by the castles and fortresses of the nobility, some of them vast and elaborate structures. Their ruins are to be found in remote parts, still guarding in lonely grandeur the strategic routes of a bygone age. The rich and powerful also built fortified residences inside the towns, one of the best surviving examples being the castles of the counts of Flanders in Ghent. The burgesses, too, were proud to expend their wealth in the building of fine stone guild halls and town houses. The technical resources available to the architects and builders were fairly simple; manpower was the chief element in all these great

206

207 208

209

operations, as indeed one would expect.

To the modern observer, the height of the medieval structures probably causes the most surprise. Wooden scaffolding was sometimes used, but more often the builders supported the scaffolding on poles let into the completed portions of the wall (206, 207). For lifting the great blocks of stone the principle of the pulley and the windlass (208) was known from a fairly early period, and later, when the crank had been invented (209), it came to displace the capstan windlass. Stone was the material chosen for the finest buildings, although many splendid wooden frame structures were built as well. We can gain some idea of the construction methods used from these illustrations of the building of Noah's Ark (210), and the building of a tower under the supervision of a prince (211). These pictures are allegorical, but quite realistic.

210

211

Large constructions were built only under the patronage of the great. A prince is seen inspecting the work of his architects (212). The building trade employed many skills. Some, such as the carpenters (214), slaters (215), and tilers (216), tended to remain resident in one town. They had their own trade associations, which formed part of the guild organization of the city. But the elite among the building workers were the masons (213, 217). Working in stone demanded high professional expertise, and it was a skill far less frequently called on than that of the worker in wood. The latter could expect to find many regular and profitable commissions within the town and its environs. The masons, on the other hand, tended to move around from one part of the country to another, following the

major projects; as a result, they were free of the restrictions of the municipal authorities. But they were not without their own trade organization. Proud in the mastery of their high craft, jealous of its secrets, they were powerful enough to protect themselves in the competitive world of employment in which they worked. The masons organized themselves in associations that overran purely national and local boundaries and developed secret rituals and signs to assure the survival of their profession as a whole. Ordinary wandering artisans were liable to find themselves at the mercy of unscrupulous employers. The masons, however, free of the bonds of society that held and protected most men, set up a system that was to provide the model for the Freemasons of a later age.

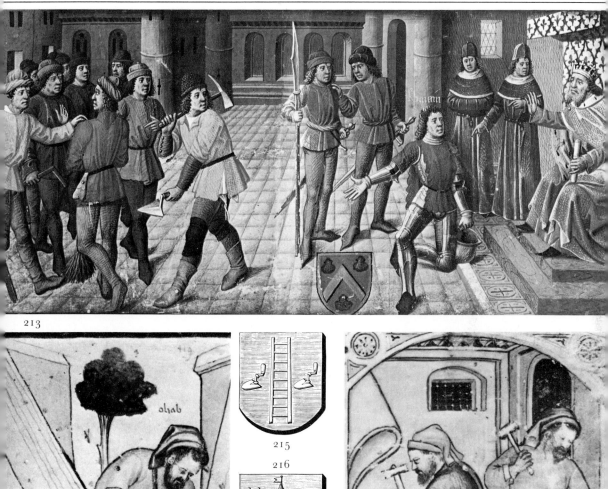

213

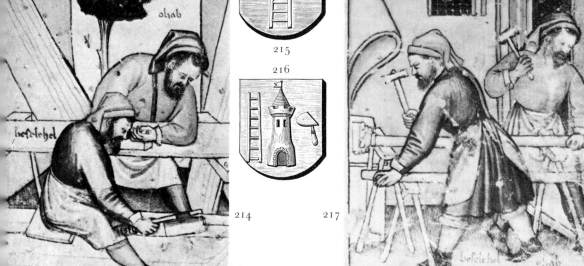

214   215   216   217

No period in the Middle Ages could match the remarkable explosion of industrial technology by our own century. Yet there were significant advances that improved and speeded production. Among the most important of these were the watermill and the invention of the windmill. These were used not only for the milling of corn, but also for industrial processes such as the fulling (whitening) of cloth. With the invention of the mechanical fulling mill in the thirteenth century, the workers and the industry began to move out of the towns, where the guilds of the hand fullers had regulated the trade. Picture 218 shows the official seal of the fullers of St. Trond, France. They settled in river valleys and by the banks of the fast-flowing streams that could provide the motive power for the new machinery. Other advances in technology included the development of gear mechan-

218

219

220

221

isms. The potter's wheel, for example, formerly given its momentum by the thrust of a long pole (219), was later fitted with a treadle mechanism.

Although such mechanical technology appears primitive today, it was of major importance in the development of medieval industrial processes. Growing knowledge of the chemistry (221) of naturally occurring compounds brought important advances in the techniques of dyeing (223) and glassmaking (220). Glassmaking demanded fairly elaborate equipment, sometimes forged by the blacksmith (222), and would be carried out in a specially designed workshop. Most other manufacturing trades, such as weaving and tailoring (224), were organized as home industries. This allowed the entrepreneur to wield full control over his scattered and disorganized workers.

222

Como Beselehel e Oliab so compagno lanora el Candeliero de oro.
Como Beselehel e Oliab so compagno lanora le colone del tabernaculo.

224

223

Although weaving was often done by women (225, 226) and was regarded as one of the diversions of the great lady (227), it was the foundation on which the wealth of Flanders and cities like Florence had been built. The weavers, like all the other trades and industries, formed their own associations and guilds ruled by the wealthy masters. Figure (228) shows the seal of the clothworkers of Bruges, and (229) the banner of the weavers of Toulon in France. The weavers themselves (230), the workers who produced the finished cloth, were among one of the most powerful group of social malcontents in the history of the medieval town.

Most of the workers lived at home. The whole family was employed on some aspect of the work: the women carded the wool and spun it, and the men operated the looms. In the Medici business, all these operations were

225

226

227

supervised by factors or overseers. These men took the work out to the weavers and collected it after each stage was complete, to check the quality of the work. They also ensured that there had been no substitution of inferior materials; this was likely to occur in the weaving of rich stuffs involving the use of gold thread. The employer held a great deal of power. Often the weaver had borrowed money from him to buy the loom, and this was held as surety by the employer; his cottage might be rented from him, and the whole family was liable to the extortions of the factor and cast upon the mercy of the employer. Even in normal times, the weavers felt themselves oppressed, but in times of hardship their plight was desperate. The worst that could happen was for the supply of wool to be cut. Indian cotton (231) was known during the later Middle Ages, but English wool reigned supreme.

228

229

230

231

Despite their wealth, indeed, usually because of it, medieval towns were often pillaged in time of war. The strong walls that surrounded them served not only to keep robbers and brigands at bay, but also to house garrisons of soldiers. The success of a campaign often depended on the capture or siege of these enemy strongpoints. In defending their city against enemy troops (232), the citizens were not merely showing loyalty to their prince or king, but protecting their own property from the sack and their families from rape and death. As we have said, certain laws governed the capture of towns in war; for example, no one could bar the gates against the lawful lord. The notorious sack of Limoges during the Hundred Years War by the Black Prince is partly explained by the fact that the prince claimed that the town lay within his father's lands in France. The spoils of war were rich.

232

233

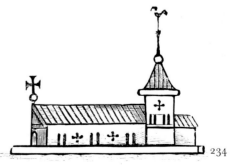

234

Even more terrible than armed sack were the horrors of the plague that regularly swept through Europe, from the first dread epidemic of the Black Death in the mid-fourteenth century. Medieval medicine, based on classical and Arabic treatises, had developed a variety of treatments (237).

But no apothecary, including Chaucer's "doctor of physic" (235), had an answer to the plague so vividly depicted in picture 236.

The only remedy, reserved to the rich, was to flee the disease-ridden city in the hope of escaping contamination and in the virtual certainty of spreading it. Other privileged groups might find refuge in one of the few medieval hospitals, endowed by great men. One was built by Henry III of England at Oxford in 1233 (234). The drawing is said to have been made by the monk-chronicler, Matthew Paris.

235

236

237

CHAPTER FOUR

GOVERNMENT AND THE ADMINISTRATION OF JUSTICE

THE KING OR THE PRINCE was the head of state, and he was expected to govern. However much the great men of the realm might wish to influence his decisions in their interests, they accepted his prerogative powers and indeed looked for him to use them. The real testing period for the medieval monarchy occurred when the king was weak or a minor. In normal times he directed the administration and, if he so willed, could achieve remarkable results, despite the limitations of the tools he had to hand. A serious difficulty of government was the poor state of most overland communications. It was hard to maintain contact with and enforce discipline on subordinate officials in the provinces. In many kingdoms, control of remoter territories had to be given up to local magnates. Even in England—the most centralized state in Europe—powerful men far from the capital, such as the Marcher lords on the frontier with Wales and the barons on the border with Scotland, could often rule their lands with virtual independence.

Side by side with the officers and organs of the royal government, there existed a whole network of ducal and lesser administrations. Often they found themselves in conflict. In terms of estate management alone, the great noble needed an army of stewards, bailiffs, and reeves. In great liberties (semi-independent regions such as the duchy of Lancaster in England and the duchy of Aquitaine in France) the ducal administration actually duplicated the royal government in most respects. Royal officials struggled hard to assert their master's authority in the territories of the powerful magnates. This is, indeed, one of the touchstones of the evolution of the modern state from its medieval forerunners. The most open conflicts occurred in territories, like Aquitaine and Gascony, where the duke happened also to be the monarch of the independent kingdom of England. This makes an illuminating study of medieval administration, for in it the modern and the medieval worlds meet. Geography, language, and history suggested that Aquitaine and Gascony were part of the kingdom of France, Paris was determined to make good its authority in these areas, and the duke kings were just as determined to resist it. Yet the conflict, which more than once exploded into full-scale war, was expressed in feudal terms, the question of the homage due from the duke to the king lay at the heart of the great Anglo-French conflict known as the Hundred Years War. The citizens of Bordeaux and the other towns of Gascony felt that English rule had too many advantages to be surrendered to the claims of "national" sentiment. The dukes spent more and more of their time ruling their English kingdom and other territories and, being anxious to retain the loyalty of their French subjects, treated them generously. The prospect of being governed from Paris, therefore became more and more distasteful. French armies finally conquered Gascony in the mid-fifteenth century and even then received only a sullen welcome.

Gascony is a good example of the problems of medieval administration. Territories with a variety of historical and governmental traditions were brought together by the dynastic marriages and the fortunes of war. Given poor communications and the strength of local traditions, outlying districts of a medieval lordship were often able to cling to their own system of law and government. Indeed, the central administration often had to abandon attempts at standardization. More often than not such an attempt was never even made. The result was an anomalous structure of administration, throughout the larger states and many lesser independent states such as the cities of northern Italy and Germany and the princely governments of Germany.

It was in the field of law that the conflict between the central and "provincial" administration was most marked. Even in England, where the advance of the central was most successful, the citizen found himself liable to many different courts for different crimes. Fairly early the crown had made good its claim to jurisdiction in all cases involving the death penalty; this, of course, included any treason against the king. But in many other smaller cases, judgment was given by the manor court, presided over by the lord of the manor. Even here, the royal courts gradually built up a system that enabled the plaintiff to take out a writ allowing him to have his case heard in the royal courts. This encroachment on their liberties caused bitter opposition

from the barons. Even the towns, the newest forces in the medieval establishment, gradually won the right to try cases relating to guild and commercial law and, like all healthy institutions, extended their field of activities. The fact that the chartered boroughs were independent of manorial jurisdiction attracted many workers from surrounding villages.

The right to hold a court was one of the most jealously prized forms of status within the feudal society. Nor was it an empty symbol. The administration of justice was a profitable business, both in legitimate fees and in the rich pickings to be made from the bribes that were commonplace. It was this as much as anything else that made royal justice so attractive to suitors. Certainly the writs cost money. But the personal interest of a royal justice in local affairs was usually slight, and the petitioner could expect a fair verdict. The determination of the royal courts to enforce a single system of justice throughout the realm extended beyond the liberties of the barons to the courts of the church. The struggle for jurisdiction over offending clerks was a fierce one. Clerks included not only the regular clergy, but also a host of men in lesser orders, who preferred the church for their master, rather than the king. Here was the heart of the bitter dispute between Henry II of England and his proud archbishop, Thomas à Becket of Canterbury—a dispute which ended with the murder of Becket in his own cathedral.

Medieval justice in all its operations was stained by the atrocities of the torturer and the brutalities of the executioners. But it was one of the achievements of the Middle Ages that the principle of equality before the law slowly became established, even if it was not always clear which law.

94   In the Middle Ages, men were subject to a variety of jurisdictions. The highest court in the land was that of the king in his council, flanked by his nobles and served by a body of skilled lawyers and clerks (238). The monarch might hear petitions from the greatest in the land (239, 241), but his jurisdiction did not extend over all cases or over all his subjects. At the start of our period, in most European monarchies, some powerful dukes and nobles had the right to hold a court free from interference by the king's justice. In England the royal courts managed to press their claims against these lesser jurisdictions at a fairly early date. Elsewhere, however, the process took much longer. In the Holy Roman Empire, for example, the central authority never won preeminence. A manuscript drawing of Henry II of England doing justice at the town gate (240) expresses the idea that royal

justice was available to all men. All too often, however, the king's lesser subjects had no appeal from the partial judgments meted out to them by their immediate lords.

The most prized possession of many a monastic house or lay tenant was the written document confirming some grant or granting some privilege given by the king or lord and authorized by his personal seal. The seal of the Canterbury monks in England is shown in picture 242. As the Middle Ages progressed, the idea grew that a document was the ultimate authorization of any claim. A grant made in public, by the exercise of a right "from time immemorial" was no longer a full guarantee. Seals became in themselves the symbol of authority and legality. This charter, making a grant of land to the English Abbey of Bury St. Edmunds in 1210, carries the seals of the Abbey and of its abbot (243).

239

240

242

241

243

Outside England great lords continued to exercise considerable rights of jurisdiction. The court (244) and seignorial government had officers in the local districts of the dukedom or principality that imitated the titles and functions of the royal administrators. More and more these rival authorities came into conflict. In France, for example, cases tried in the seignorial court often came to be referred to, and accepted by, the royal *parlement* at Paris for appeals. In an extreme case the monarch might be forced to go to war to defend his claims against a powerful vassal.

As the central administration gradually made headway against the aristocratic courts, it had to take account of the growth of a new type of jurisdiction—that of the towns. In England the position was weighted against the local authority. The town gained the enjoyment of its privileges through the grant of a

244

245

246

247

royal charter. Although the power and prestige of the mayors of London like Richard Whittington (246) were real and the capital dared to oppose the royal wishes, this was very much the exception to the rule. However great their pride in their city, Londoners had no tradition of semi-independence from higher authority that lay behind the great seal of continental towns like the Flemish city of Ypres (245).

Minor town courts were concerned with lesser offences such as the domestic problem of the nagging wife. Many a parish court had its own array of scolds' bridles, like this one (248). August courts, such as the provosts of the merchants of Paris (249), dealt with complex cases of commercial law, settled many lesser criminal actions, and regulated city tolls for the maintenance of the approach roads and bridges (247) and rental of market space.

248

249

The Middle Ages had high ideals of justice and probity, illustrated by this allegory of the "Provident Household" (250). The steward "Circumspection" is assisted by the seneschal (steward) "Reason" on his right, and the commander of the armed forces "Discretion" on his left. The other officers of the household are "Intellect," "Economy," "Deliberation," and "Harmony." But of course, the ideal was often betrayed. Judicial penalties were often crude, when not brutal; for giving false measure or using debased metals the trader or master craftsman might be pilloried (251) by the city court, no light punishment. Such cases fell within the jurisdiction of the borough courts or might even concern royal justices. For other crimes—adultery and insolence to authority—the age-old penalty was the stocks (254).

The most brutal weapon of the medieval

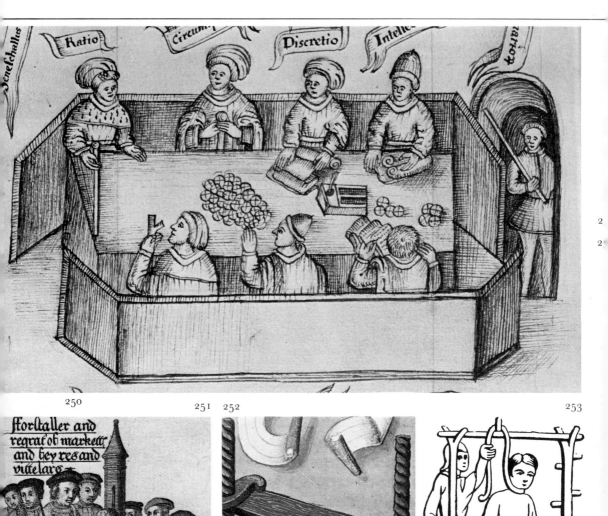

250

251 252

253

fforstaller and regrator of markett and bey res and vittelars

torturer was *peine forte et dure*, in which the offender was crushed to death (252). This form of death could be chosen by traitors who wished to save their family from disinheritance.

Death by decapitation, rather than by hanging (253), was the privilege of noblemen. In public the façade of the established order was held together by such means, but in the privacy of the "examination" room no victim was protected from the refined sadism that was the well-paid torturer's stock-in-trade. In light of the illustrations on these pages, it is hard to know whether the brutality itself or the presence of the robed judge and his recording clerk (255) is more repugnant. In a world where brutality and violence were commonplace, torture was a recognized means of "obtaining information", and part of the rough pattern of justice which characterized the Middle Ages.

Between the lord and the peasant there was, of course, a series of intermediate officials from the steward, who was the estate manager, down to the lord's bailiff, whose job was to supervise the work done on the estate. In conjunction with the manor reeve, the bailiff had to ensure that every tenant did the requisite number of days' work on the manor lands. The reeve was often recruited from the higher ranks of the local peasantry and was one of the officials of the manor court. As can be imagined, he was not always the most popular member of the local community.

The daily life of the common people was carried on in the shadow of authority. It was carried on, too, under the shadow of the castles of the great (256), rising proudly over the surrounding countryside. These great fortresses were a constant reminder to the toiling peasants of where real power lay. Of all the

256

laws to which the peasant was subject, probably those governing the forests and the wildlife in them were the most irksome and severe. Huge tracts of wooded country and moorland were set apart as royal forests and dedicated to serving the royal passion for the chase. Much more of Europe was forested in the Middle Ages than is today. The local population was liable to the most brutal and summary penalties for the poaching of game and was pre-vented from enclosing or cultivating land or otherwise interfering with the habitat of the wild animals. The huntsmen (257, 258) had absolute rights of riding and hawking over these lands. The high place enjoyed in the social order by the servants of the kings is symbolized by the magnificent tomb erected to the memory of the thirteenth century master of the royal hunt William Malgeneste, represented here (259).

257

258

259

CHAPTER FIVE
THE LIFE OF THE PEOPLE

THE THEME OF THIS BOOK has been the life of those in authority in town and countryside. The acts of popes and kings, bishops and princes and the display and wealth of the great merchants are the subjects which once claimed the attention of most historians. No doubt, for the people of the time, doings of the great and powerful were the events of real importance. The recent work of some historians in analyzing and describing the structure of society at all levels has done much to redress the balance. But as we turn now to look at the lives of ordinary folk, we should not forget that bitterly as they may sometimes have resented their lot, they knew that the system would always enclose their lives. Sometimes they aimed to force concessions from those in authority, but they could not have hoped for much.

At the base of the agricultural community lay the institution of serfdom. It had its origins in an earlier age, when its conditions could be willingly accepted in return for positive advantages. By the later Middle Ages, however, it had become rigid and oppressive. Despite its name, serfdom was not slavery; slaves were known in medieval Europe, but they were usually non-Christian prisoners of war. In earlier centuries serfs had had and had exercised the right to hold land. A serf might be a prosperous man, more prosperous indeed than neighbors with the status of freemen. But his status had one vital disability—the serf was bound to the land. He could not, without the permission of his lord, move out of the lord's jurisdiction into the services of another. This permission was rarely granted. Furthermore, the condition of serfdom was marked by the annual payment of a small amount of head money. This was a paltry sum, but an unmistakable symbol of servitude—and it was hereditary. A man might voluntarily surrender his freedom, but neither he nor his descendants could of their own will rid themselves of the stigma of serfdom. In the expanding and fluid social conditions of the eleventh century, men had voluntarily given themselves into the serfdom and their descendants. One man doubled his holding by an extra vineyard, and since he had no intention of moving from this little estate and could see no reason why his children should wish to, the bargain must have seemed a good one. But by the fourteenth century conditions had changed. With the commutation, in some regions, of work services for money, workers demanded the liberty of movement to take advantage of these higher rates elsewhere; it was now that resignation of his freedom by a remote ancestor really took its effect. A man born into an unfree family was himself unfree, unless formally given back his liberty by his lord. In the latter part of the fourteenth century, however, few landlords were anxious to free men from obligations to work on their estates. The dreadful epidemic known as the Black

Death killed, it has been estimated, about one-third of the population of Europe. No social class escaped, but it was, of course, the decimation of the work force that affected the wealth and power of the territorial magnates. There was now a premium on the price of employment as landowners competed for the help of peasants from other parts of the country even while, at the same time, trying to enforce the full conditions of serfdom against their own tenants.

The fourteenth century was indeed a time of turmoil among the lower orders of society. In England the great Peasants' Revolt seemed for a moment to bring the whole establishment of church and state to the brink of anarchy; the part played by the boy King Richard is one of the famous, though perhaps not creditable, episodes of English history. Royal promises freely made for the occasion were freely broken when the danger was past. Yet the outbreak was not one of great violence; it was a protest against unjust taxation and against the efforts of landlords to reimpose already outdated obligations of tenure. Of course, the revolt gave vent to bitter and long-repressed discontent with the general injustices of the social condition; the peasants of 1381 were not the first, nor were to be the last, to pose the old riddle:

When Adam delved and Eve span,
Who was then the Gentleman?

The attack was directed primarily against the manorial records. There was none of the senseless, brutal rape and killing that characterized the rising of the Jacquerie in France and the horrific vengeance exacted by the nobles in their turn. But these two incidents reveal that below the surface was an ever-present threat to the members of the establishment. Such ex-plosions were rare; the system was too effective and the resources of privilege and power too great to permit many outbreaks.

Kings and rulers in Europe were confronted by a number of revolts of towns and burgesses that overturned the proper order of things in the most direct way on the battlefield. The century opened with the victory of the Flemish cities over the chivalry of France at the Battle of Courtrai in 1302. The men of Flanders enjoyed other victories, and their presumption was not to be finally punished for another eighty years. In Switzerland, the newly independent countrymen and citizens of the independent cantons were proving their superiority to the mounted knights of Austria with some regularity. In the fourteenth century we can begin to disconcern cracks in the façade of authority.

More than a century later, the peasantry in England and certain other parts of Western Europe had shaken off the worst oppressions of serfdom. While the old establishment of clergy and aristocracy had fended off the sometimes serious threats of social turmoil, they, too, had had to embrace a new element in the shape of powerful merchant princes. In Italy these men won the status of independent rulers, and everywhere proved to be indispensable sources of revenue for the church.

The balance of social power, if one may use the term, had shifted at the top, and movement had begun in the lower reaches that was to have long-term effects. Yet although the peasant had his joys and pleasures, for the most part his lot was one of poverty and oppression. It was his shoulders that supported the magnificence of the privileged classes.

The contrast between the life of the peasant and his lord could hardly be better summed up than by the two illustrations on this page. The artist who portrayed the magnificence of Babylon (260) drew on his experiences of the powerful and wealthy of his own day. The technique he used, providing a cross section, so to speak, of the castle, is a perfect image of the noble landowner, the focus of the life on the estates that provided his riches. Another artist drew the charming vignette shown in picture 261 at the foot of a manuscript page. It shows the other side of the coin. The peasant sits on a stool before the fire; he has taken his boots off to dry his feet after a hard day's work in the wet fields and is serving himself the watery broth in the pot on the fire.

The ploughman working in the fields (263) is

260

262

261

using the heavy plough developed in the tenth century, which in its various forms revolutionized the agriculture of northern Europe. By using a heavy shear and colter board to turn over the soil, it tilled deeper than earlier types and aerated the soil more thoroughly. The result was more fertile and productive land. Together with the introduction of rich protein crops, such as beans, the general diet of the European peasant was enriched, a factor which seems to have been an important one in the population explosion during the eleventh century. Peasants gathered the harvest under the supervision of the lord's bailiff (262).

Picture 264 shows the appearance of a French peasant of the thirteenth century, carrying a hoe and water gourd.

263

264

Despite their exalted position, the members of the medieval nobility were familiar with the life on their estates and seem to have been interested in it. A well-run estate was a source both of satisfaction and of wealth and power. Where conditions were good, a magnate could feel that he was fulfilling his stewardship to the many men and women who depended on his lands and his justice. On a practical level, a magnate could place more reliance on his tenants in time of war and political upheaval.

Many of the illustrations in this section come from the richly decorated books of devotion produced under landowners' patron-

265

266

age; a favourite topic was the farmer's work as it changed from season to season—showing ploughing, harrowing, and sowing. Other subjects illustrated included peasants eating their lunch during the harvest (265), at work on the threshing floor (266), or shearing sheep (267). One of the most famous of these illustrated books of devotion is the psalter illuminated for the Luttrell family of Lincolnshire. Our pictures from it show ploughing with a team of oxen and the heavy plough (268) and harrowing the fields at seedtime (269); the slinger following the harrow is doing his best to drive away the crows that are plundering the farmer's seed.

267

268

269

The peasant's life was a hard one, but it was not without its compensations. The agricultural year had its great festivals with dancing and music, some of them of a semi-pagan origin. But apart from these landmarks, the lowest classes of society had to make their own entertainments. Sophisticated pastimes such as chess, chivalric diversions, and reading were quite beyond their experience. For the most part, they took their pleasures from the land on which they had their bare existence. Sometimes cockfights were staged (270), affording a rather savage and primitive outlet and an opportunity for gambling. Rabbit

270

271

hunting (271) was another sport—illicit, because it involved theft of a lord's property. Not as grand or spectacular as hawking or stag hunting with hounds, it nevertheless provided recreation and a chance to satisfy a starved appetite. Another similar sport, easily managed by the poor, was hunting birds with a sling and stone (273), although this, too, would often involve poaching and severe penalties if the offender was brought before his lord's bailiff. Apart from such pastimes, the only recreations the peasant classes had in an endless battle against nature and their betters arose from customary social life (272).

272

273

A charming portrayal of ploughing and sowing is seen in picture 277. Oxen, not horses, are used for the plough teams. Overlooking the field is the comfortable half-timbered home of the small tenant farmer for whom these peasants work. Figure (275) shows a peasant scything the corn.

The introduction of the windmill in the eleventh and twelfth centuries was an important advance since it brought a new source of mechanical power to the countryside. The watermill (274) was still more useful, in countries with swift-flowing streams, since it did not depend on the vagaries of the weather. Watermills were used for mechanical fulling and a variety of purposes besides the milling of wheat. Their exploitation was an important prelude to the Industrial Revolution of later centuries, and wherever they were set up, they gathered around them a cluster of houses and

276

274

275

often prompted significant shifts in population and industrial activity. It was the use of waterpower for fulling that led to the concentration of the English cloth industry in the western and northwestern parts of the country. The fast-running streams of the Yorkshire dales and the west country were ideal for the purpose, and other branches of the industry tended to follow where the fullers were established. It was also in these regions that some of the best sheep were to be found so that the sources both of the raw material and of the power were conveniently centralized. The wool industry (276) was vital to the economy of medieval England and was the characteristic rural industry of that country.

In France the cultivation of the vine held an equivalent position. French winemaking is illustrated and described on the following two pages.

277

The grand tradition of French winemaking has been traced back to the vineyards established by the Romans. In the Middle Ages the export wine trade became an important source of revenue, and then, as now, England was France's best customer. For a long period, Gascony was part of the domain of the King of England, and the convenient import situation that resulted helped establish the Englishman's tradition—a love of claret. The fine vintage was the pride of the rich man's table. From the cutting of the grapes in the vineyard (279) to the laying down of the wine in the large resinated wooden casks (278) little has changed in the business of making a great wine. If a winepress is now more general than the age-old

278

279

method of treading the grapes (280, 282), the modern worker in a vineyard is as likely as his medieval predecessor to help himself occasionally to a bunch of grapes, like these two vintagers of thirteenth-century Brussels (281). Another more significant change is the way in which the wine was sold to the customer. All possible care was lavished on ensuring the correct temperature and other conditions necessary for the maturing of a fine vintage at the château itself. The modern phrase "château bottled," however, would have been unknown in those days. Those merchants or nobles who were rich enough to insist on the best would, as a rule, buy their wine by the cask from a merchant or shipper.

280

281

282

Winemaking was probably the most specialized of the agricultural skills, but the art of the beekeeper (284) was only slightly less complex and certainly as important. Although sugar was imported from the East, its price was prohibitive for the average man, whose only other sweetener was honey. The vast majority of those who worked on the land were farmers and the peasants (283). Their tools, although simple by modern standards, called for expertise in both their manufacture and their maintenance. The smith was a skilled ironworker and one of the most important members of the community (285, 286). Hoes, pruning hooks, axes, knives, sheep shearers, and, above all, the heavy plough had to be serviced and maintained. In a society where the horse was a major source of power, as well

283

284

285

as the only means of transport, the smith was bound to be prosperous. Like the miller, he was not averse to sharp practice. One method of turning a dishonest penny was to drive a fine nail into the hoof as he fitted a new shoe for the horse of any unwary visitor. A mile or two down the road the horse would go lame. At this point the visitor at a loss for transport, would be met by a cooperative rustic with a serviceable nag that he would offer in exchange for the gentleman's splendid but unfortunately useless horse. The deal was struck, and the peasant hastened back to his colleague in the smithy, who extracted the nail and a week or two later, after resting the horse, sold it for a healthy profit to the next person who was passing by, and who found himself in similar "difficulties."

The men of the Middle Ages did not view petty dishonesty with the same astonishment as our gentler generation. Social injustice could be seen on every hand. The worker on the great estate (287, 288) was obliged to give up part of his time to the tending of another man's land. Usually he received no payment for this. Even the richest peasant, farming several acres, could expect rough justice in his lord's court if he fell foul of feudal law. The towering fortified residences of the nobles were a daily reminder of life's hard realities. Corruption in high places was commonplace. Death, too, was on every hand, often pictured

in manuscript paintings and woodcuts as the officer of the last great court of judgment where every man had to render account for his stewardship in life. He is seen, too, as a warning in picture 289, one of the earliest printed woodcuts, dating from 1482 and made in Flanders. Death is represented with a great scythe, mortal men as the unwilling harvest. The idea of equality before death did not always reduce the inequalities of society, but it did offer the hope of lasting compensation, so to speak, for the troubles and hardships of the human world. Upon this hope rested much of the medieval establishment.

288
289

287

118 The basis of medieval social attitudes was twofold: the hierarchy of feudalism and the beliefs of Christianity. The ideals of knighthood included the helping of the weak, as well as the conquest of the infidel. The example of St. Martin (290), who divided his cloak with a poor man, was one of the many admonitions to generosity and humility that the church offered to the rich and powerful. The monasteries, motivated by the universal laws of hospitality and of Christian charity, also provided lodging and food to wayfarers. This scene of wayside hospitality (291) was printed by William Caxton, the first English printer, in 1483. Europe was still a hostile continent. The wasteland and forest still covered wide

290

291

tracts, in which wild animals and robbers roamed. A communal sense of self-interest, as much as any altruistic motive, prompted men to extend to one another basic hospitality. For the great, it was a sign of social status and a natural demonstration of wealth and success to give freely of their plenty (292). The vast meals apparently consumed whenever a duke or merchant sat down to table are the wonder of a later age, but a great man also had to cater for a household thronging with servants and hangers-on. Even strangers at the door could expect a good meal. The servants of one fifteenth-century duke were entitled to as much meat as they could carry away from the kitchen on their knives; a common practice.

After the terrible devastations of the plague in the fourteenth century the ever-present awareness of death became oppressive. Many manuscripts handed down to posterity portray scenes of a tragic and morbid quality. Picture 293 shows a helpless cripple, who could only hope for a miracle to cure him. Such sights were common and were a perpetual reminder of mankind's frail condition. The pomp and ceremony of a great man's life could be suddenly ended by the mortality that he shared with the humblest of his fellows. In earlier centuries, funerary monuments had portrayed him in full dress and the trappings of his earthly greatness. In the fifteenth century and later, however, artists portrayed the

293

294

naked body unadorned (294), to remind men of every rank that they left life as they had entered it. Sometimes the most extreme stages of decay were pictured, the bones starting through the decaying flesh and worms crawling from the eye sockets.

Such morbid premonitions made the parable of the rich man and the beggar potent warnings. The luxury of proud Dives in the Bible story did not save him from the horrors of hell after death; the sufferings of Lazarus, driven from his gate by the dogs set on him by the servants of the house, found ample recompense in eternal life, when he passed up to dwell in the glory of heaven (295). See, too, the story told on the next page (296).

295

Throughout the Middle Ages, then, the established and privileged classes had maintained themselves at the expense of the mass of humanity. Their privileges had been exemplified by a judicial system of one law for the great, as in this picture of a French lord being tried by his peers (297), and one for the poor; it was exemplified by the authority of the church and papacy (299) over the lay world; and it was exemplified by the monopoly of leisure and learning held by Europe's great families (298).

The close of our period was beginning to witness profound changes. The old medieval establishment was not destined to survive in its old forms. The Renaissance, with its rediscovery of the classical arts and sciences, its new challenges, and its new means of spreading ideas through printing presses, was to bring about a revolution in European society.

296

It was true that ordinary people would continue to live hard lives under the shadow of authority—but the nature of that authority was changing. The power of the papacy was to be further eroded by the work of sixteenth-century reformers personified by Martin Luther, and its place increasingly taken by the reformed churches throughout Europe. The place of the nobility in the establishment, too, was to change, as feudal forms of land-holding were modified by economic pressures. Much of the new initiative was to be taken by Europe's major towns, ruled by rising merchant groups, who in their turn would achieve greater prominence in national government, and create a new and powerful mercantile establishment. These and many other changes played a part in changing the society of Europe, and men began to look upon the medieval establishment as a bygone order.

297

298

299

FURTHER READING

The Life of the Merchants

M. V. Clarke, *The Medieval City State* (London, 1926)
I. Origo, *Merchant of Prato* (London, 1957)
R. de Roover, *The Rise and Decline of the Medici Bank* (London, 1963)

The Life of the Nobility

Joseph Calmette, *The Golden Age of Burgundy* (1949; English translation, London, 1962)
N. Denholme Young, *History and Heraldry*
Kenneth Fowler, *The Age of Plantagenet and Valois* (London, 1969)
Geoffrey Hindley, *Castles of Europe* (London, 1968)
M. H. Keen, *The Laws of War in the Later Middle Ages* (London, 1965)
Gervase Mathew, *The Court of Richard II* (London, 1968)
Margaret Wade Labarge, *A Baronial Household of the 13th Century* (London, 1965)

General

Marc Bloch, *Feudal Society* (London, 1965)
Joan Evans, *The Flowering of the Middle Ages* (London, 1966)
Friedrich Heer, *The Medieval World* (London, 1962)
J. Huizinga, *The Waning of the Middle Ages* (English translation, London, 1924)
R. W. Southern, *The Making of the Middle Ages* (London, 1953)

PICTURE CREDITS

INDEX